Passion, Prayer, and Purpose

A Collection of Stories to Help Any Woman

Design + Her + Life

By:

Nicole Sallis and Consuela Cooper

Dedication

This book, born from a place of darkness and despair, is dedicated to any woman attempting to find herself, start anew, or break the chains that have been holding her back. Our hope is, that as you read each story, you find confirmation, comfort, and strength and that, as you go through the workbook, you begin to develop a renewed sense of self-esteem, self-awareness, and self-love that only comes from within.

Acknowledgements

Thank you to our contributors who believed in our dream and put their fears aside to write stories that may have been painful to reflect on. We thank you for being vulnerable and using your struggles, journeys, and successes to help another beautiful woman find the strength and courage to
Design + Her + Life

A special thank you to:
Dr. Novella Washington, Editor
Donnie Rogers, Cover Design

Table of Contents

Introduction

Why Passion, Prayer, and Purpose

Design + Her + Life

The birth of a movement.

Nicole Sallis

Passion

Stories on how finding your passion fuels you each day despite the challenges that come with it.

Keep Your Head Up and Your Heart Strong:Zina Lanay

Entrepreneurship:LaRicia Nelson

Finding My Purpose:Victoria Ross

The Power of Choice:Thoko Spoon

Passion Leads to Purpose:Kelly McHenry

Setbacks Are Setups(For Greatness):Susan Higgins

Workbook: Design

Prayer

Stories on the power and importance of alone time with God and yourself.

Power, Perks, and Purpose of Prayer:Priscilla Green

Finding God in Myself (and I Loved Her):Samora Suber

Sweet Hour of Prayer:Consuela Cooper

Workbook: Her

Purpose

Stories about using life's pains to NOT define you but MOVE you to the greatness God created you for.

The Reality of Happiness: Jamie Berry

The Art of Healing: Frances Bradley

The Case of the Ex: Keyaira Phillips

The Road to Myself: Sophia Nicole

Overcoming Challenges: Danessa Seward

Workbook: Life

Bonus Track: Letters to My Younger Self

Reflection is the most important part of the learning process.

Karayan Willis

Ashley Caldwell

Tammy Gardner

Maureen Saturne

Kateea Scott

Tanara Lynnece

Introduction

Dear Reader,

Congratulations on taking the first step at Designing Your Life! The journey you are about to embark upon will take you through the lives of twenty women who have used their pain to launch them into their passion while they fulfill their God given purpose. While all stories vary in nature, from the background of the author to the path life has taken them on, we guarantee you will identify with each author in some way. As you read each story, your mind may begin to think about things you want to do differently, new goals you want to set, hobbies you realize you can turn into a paycheck, or old dreams you now wish to revisit. The workbook exercise(s) placed at the end of each chapter are designed to help you organize your thoughts and reconnect with yourself as you Design+Your+Life.

Thank you for your purchase, we pray this book blesses you as it has us.

With love,

Nicole Sallis + Consuela Cooper

Design + Her + Life

The Birth of a Movement

I want my Greatness

Have you ever had an inkling you were meant for something significant? That you have yet to really tap into the fullest of your God-given greatness? I don't know about you, but I ask myself these questions all the time. I would wake up regularly while I was in college with a shortness of breath, praying that I could tap into a perceived greatness I felt deep inside of me but it was like I just didn't have the roadmap to locate it, know how to reach it, or operate consistently in it. How can I show up in the world as powerful as I feel inside, the woman God says I am? How can I show up every single day as "fearfully and wonderfully made" as I am spoken of in the beautiful writings of Psalm 139?

My college years were a difficult time for my family and I, so when I finally received my degree it was such a meaningful accomplishment. However, as an aspiring fashion designer, I had pursued every fashion opportunity I could find in Iowa at the time and I needed more! Like every graduate I felt the anxiety of navigating the real world. There would be no campus, student loans or adviser to help you find growth opportunities. What would be my career move after college? My heart was set on going to New York City. Like many, I had been enamored with the big city since I was a child, reading about the trendy upscale boutiques off Fifth Ave, the art galleries of Soho, the elaborate fabric store in the fashion district and the white tents in Bryant Park for Fashion Week. As a young aspiring Fashion Designer there was nowhere to be but New York City. As a child I would find fashion inspiration and search for ways to get these ideas out of my mind and into the world. My ideas were bitter sweet most of the time; I was fascinated with my dream innovations but often times frustrated if I couldn't find a way for my creative ideas to be fully expressed. I attempted to use visual art, sketching by hand, even on computer and I begged my grandmother to teach me how to sew. So graduation day was my long awaited chance to intentionally explore my

fashion career aspirations, to find my tribe, and to unleash some of my own deeply suppressed levels of creative genius. It didn't matter what I needed to sacrifice, sell my car and all my belongings, learn a new intimidating city alone, or sleep on the street, all things I did by the way, I was willing to do whatever necessary to be successful. I was moving to attain more than a career. I wanted my door, my runway and my opportunity to expound my personal poten¬tial far beyond mediocrity. I wanted my big shot at the buzzer (that I've been working countless hours in the gym on) … I WANTED MY GREATNESS.

Nerves of Steel

My first experience living in New York was while I was still in college. I took a year off from school in Iowa and decided I would move to Brooklyn to intern with a popular fashion brand. There weren't a lot of opportunities in Iowa for fashion at the time and internship opportunities certainly didn't come easy. I actually planned a trip to the Magic Trade Show the year prior, with the clear intention of networking with a fashion professional or two. I wasn't a fashion company or a buyer so I ended up sneaking into the convention center where the show was taking place in hopes of networking with someone, anyone, that could help me get into the fashion scene in New York City. I walked around for hours, I finally met a few professional designers, so I pulled out my portfolio and pitched myself. My portfolio was not very good by the way. It consisted of actual pictures of clothing I had previously designed and sewed, I did not realize that it needed technical packages, CADs (computer aid designs) and more

but I didn't let that stop me. I consistently followed up with the few professionals that I met for the entire year. I taught myself one of the most commonly used computer programs in the industry, sent emails, followed up, sent more emails and finally landed an internship opportunity with a popular clothing company in New York. I worked high-end retail to save enough money to be able to afford to spend the summer in New York with no family, no professional network and no financial support. My father insisted on driving me 24 hours to New York to work for the summer to gain experience. When I caught my first sight of the Manhattan skyline in the warm sunset, I was driving in the car with my father I felt like I couldn't breathe, "what have I gotten myself into?" I thought. But I was determined to have fluidity in the face of change even if I couldn't predict what that change was going to look like. I had a relationship with God and together we could figure out my living situation, the awkwardness of not having one friend in the city, navigating extensive subway systems, whatever I needed to do to make it through this summer even in spite of my fear. It was probably one of the scariest but best learning experiences of my life, it was amazing and exhilarating summer that showed me the strength of my own will to make things happen. The summer internship confirmed what I initially thought, now I was certain, New York was where I wanted to be! When I returned to Iowa for the next semester of college I was so inspired with a renewed sense of direction and determination. The experience in New York definitely deepened my relationship with God, it felt like I was constantly required to step out on faith. I also came back to Iowa with more personal and creative confidence and I was persistently putting my design work out in the world. Local newspapers and the school website began to write stories about my collections and inquire about my shows.

Numerous organizations requested new, bigger, and bet¬ter fashion segments and entire shows for their events. I dreaded coming back to college after my internship but could justify the decision. I worked very hard through such a difficult personal season for my degree, and on graduation day, I was not only overjoyed and proud of myself, I knew that I was going back to New York to land my first professional fashion job! Most of my circle of friends saw me as the one who was going to make things happen, the one who searched for every opportunity to prove the naysayers wrong. I was the person who relished in the opportunities by raising her hand to go first, the one seemingly unafraid to try something new or always ready to zip-line down the mountain. I was the person from small-town Waterloo, Iowa that sacrificed everything to pursue a career in fashion in a crazy new city. "Nerves of steel" is how my mother referred to me.

30 + No Job

The year I turned 30, I was satisfied with many aspects of my life. I had been enthusiastically living the last seven years in New York City, fulfilling my youthful dreams of working in the Fashion Industry and much more.

Worked as a celebrity stylist. Check.

Giving Back. I was offering my time, volunteering weekly for my church doing wardrobes styling and writing. Check.

Landed multiple professional fashion design jobs with well-known brands. Check.

Used my poetry and writing to inspire women across the country in ways beyond my wildest dreams…Madison Square Garden. Check.

Wrote and published a book. Check

Used my influence and passions to inspire youth in my hometown of Waterloo, Iowa. Check.

Started a foundation to creatively empower communities around the country. Check

I wasn't just achieving goals, I was in a great place spiritually, serving, studying, praying and consistently talking to God. I was now expanding from a social perspective, frequenting Designer Sample Sales, Broadway plays, and my favorite recording artists' album release parties. I was indulging in culturally diverse food options, a youthful cool church, benefit concerts at Carnegie Hall and a few New York Knicks even showed up to my book release party. I wasn't just treading swamp water; I was doing a beautiful backstroke in my childhood dreamland of New York City. Although, at times, it was a laborious, difficult journey…I was living!

So why was I crying every day before my 30th birthday?

Well, this wasn't how I was telling my story. My story wasn't checks and life balances…it was struggle after struggle, from financial to exhaustion to growing insecurity. I was secretly losing my personal and professional confidence and before I knew it I was drowning in overtaking water currents of fear. I had just recently been laid off from a fashion company that decided to close the entire division where I was working.

Getting laid off wasn't uncommon to most people I knew in the fashion industry. What they don't show on the big screen at fashion week is that this industry is less of a creative romantic and more of a heart wrenching roller coaster. Most of the designers I knew loved their creative ex¬pression moments. However, we all dreaded the post-recession risk adverse buyer or production meetings where designers are asked to basically knock off their 8 bestselling styles from last year in new colors, which basically leaves some designers' roles and work obsolete. Every stylist I knew loved the fringe benefits of working with celebrities but hated the inconsistency and chasing networks or artist managers around for their checks to make rent. The entertainment and fashion industries are exciting but volatile at times and for the first time it hit me hard. Initially I thought I would be excited about the idea of not having a day job because I wouldn't have to juggle my other aspirations. I could take time off to rest and realign my focus but after about two weeks at home, I did not know what to do with myself. I started crying and couldn't stop. All I could think of was, "here I am, 30 years old in New York with no family, no husband, no kids and now, no job."

30 + Losing myself to Societal Pressure

Turning 30 was about a distinct story for me, a narrative I didn't even realize had made such an impression on me until I hit this wall in my career. The narrative was I was supposed to have it all together by 30, the house, the investments, the beautiful family, the amazing husband and the purposeful, successful career! I didn't have it all together and I wasn't even close. It was no ones' fault but mine that I ended up here, in this unsettled and unhappy position. How did I get here? I couldn't answer and I just couldn't wrap my mind around my feeling about my outcome. I was the one who always following her heart, was my heart wrong? I always followed my spirit even when it wasn't popular, was my spirit wrong? I tried so hard, so intentionally to follow every single thing God had been leading me to do even when it was uncomfortable or inconvenient. I was abstaining from sex, I had been waiting on my husband, love, connection, intimacy for 5 years. I was in every service, donated a percentage of every dime and devoted all my free time to causes close to my heart. I prayed and encouraged so many people to trust the process and God's timing. I would fast and pray before I proceeded with the career moves, any opportunities, even entertaining friendships. I felt like God had somehow forgotten me, I was the one left with no peace, no joy, no greatness, no happy-ending.

The truth is, my life looked exciting on the outside (and honestly it was at times) however, I was devastatingly exhausted. My (9 to 5) Designer position was already more like a 9am to 11pm position when we had a deadline, which was most of the time. Styling freelance. Serving at my church on Fridays and Saturdays. Working on a book. Hosting a weekly fellowship for Christians in the entertainment industry every Tuesday. Trying to run a foundation (with little to no experience but a great vision) was starting to affect my relationship with a close friend/business partner. The list went on and on. Even though I found satisfaction in my passion for creativity, fashion, personal and spiritual development, I wasn't working efficiently and truly burning the candle at both ends, as my Father would say. I had so much on my plate it was impossible to give 100% to anything. Doing all the tasks I thought God was leading me to do but I was feeling completely overwhelmed and I had become resentful with God and myself. My narrative started to change to what I now call a limiting belief, "Maybe I'm not ____ enough for the life I truly desire". Those blanks were filled with statements of self-doubt; maybe I was not strong enough to have it all, to be the career woman, wife, and mother I once dreamed of. Now I was supposed to be ready to add a huge thing like a family to that plate? The biggest problem for me is that I wasn't there yet; I was so far from my greatness in my mind. I spent my 20s building up my career by trying to get experience and credibility, only to feel that a life decision had to be made. Here I was with a career path primarily limited to the New York area. Yes, I was enjoying some of the fruit to the lifestyle as a single woman in this city working in the entertainment industry. However, my upbringing in Iowa was really kicking it on multiple levels and I couldn't imagine integrating a family into this crazy environment.

So I wasn't just dealing with the magical switch that apparently flips when the clock strikes midnight on your 30th Birthday. I was conflicted with the idea that I needed to be in New York to grow my career and didn't want to raise my family there. The recurring question constantly surfaced in my mind, "Can I really have it ALL… everything I desire, a great career and a great family?" I was so diverged and confused. From the personal perspective, I missed my family. They were my support system, even from a distance. I am a very family-oriented person and the distance was starting to wear on me. Truthfully, I wasn't ready to have children so this made me question if I had real deep psychological issues around motherhood. My biological clock, society, church and everyone around me was telling me I was supposed to be ready and I just wasn't. Was I just enormously selfish or was it something wrong with me?

Honestly speaking I was terrified of relationships, I had become a coward when it came to love, too afraid of getting hurt, I couldn't commit to the constant vulnerability and willingness to connect that loving someone requires. In fact, I had not been in a committed relationship in so many years when I slowed down with my career, I realized I was deeply lonely. I wanted something real. Deep inside I wanted connection, something more than the games I created to keep me safe. I developed an entire system to try and keep myself from falling in love (which never works) but it was an idea of "fragmented companionship"- a system where you use different people for different needs getting just close enough to feel a type of connection while never exposing yourself or getting vulnerable enough to experience an authentic loving relationship or more importantly get hurt. I had gotten to a place in my life where the fear of getting hurt outweighed the perceived benefit of a loving relationship. So I was really struggling yet feeling the pres¬sure from every angle. I have never experienced pressure like this before or been asked so much about my relationship status. From the torrent of unsolicited pep talks about finding a man and having children from co-workers, to being questioned by family member like I went against a type of moral obligation because I was putting my career over marriage to the most popular from my church community members' attitudes about single women over 30 "If you're really virtuous, why hasn't anyone found you yet?". As if being a single Black Christian woman in her 30's suggests that I haven't done something right along the way or well enough to become a wife. Singleness is too often seen as an unfortunately consequence. As if I needed an explanation of why I was living as an individual and not as part of a couple.

I think that we are socialized to believe we should feel lonelier and remorseful in our 30's if you're ambitious and not married. Women are made to feel like we're not living our life the right way until we've found another person to validate our own existence. We are socialized through media messages, school instruction, family expectations, experiences in the workplace and growing up. For example, I took Home Economics in grade school and learned about gender roles and what

I'm supposed to be doing as a woman. I started playing house with Barbie and Ken's family at 4 years old. Barbie was fashionably fly as I used all my grandmothers' high-end fabrics to design her custom wardrobe. She was a Designer and a Mom with a giant, beautiful playhouse, 2 luxury cars, 3 adorable children, and a pink, plastic pet dog. These are a couple examples, so keep in mind the clock wasn't just biological, but emotional, social, cultural and most of all arduous. All of a sudden my Barbie dreams didn't seem realistic anymore. Don't forget I was in church every Sunday and I had heard the term submission so much; all I could think about was how contradicting these ideas seemed to how powerfully I wanted to show up in the world and it just didn't seem to fit my ambitions.

Unfortunately, "The cultural story of good mothering has not been reconciled yet to reflect working women," says now Facebook COO Sheryl Sandberg. Sandberg definitely captured an aspect of reality of career minded women in our society and the internal struggle I was facing. Yes, modern day women have more options than ever before; however, women are often times still plagued with unrealistic home expectations and primary childcare responsibilities while trying to maintain demanding careers. Furthermore, with the ever-rising cost of living unlike the 1940s and 1950s working was more of a necessity, than passion for a career choice. Most of the career-focused men, who possessed the qualities I was attracted to, were all expressively clear that they were looking for a woman who was willing to put everything else on the back burner to take care of them and the kids. The men I was meeting were all attracted to my strength and ambition in theory but wanted me to just turn all of that off if we decided to move forward and be serious. Women are often made to feel like a successful career, leadership roles or implementing our passions are just temporary fillers until we find a significant other who will take their place. Women's creative and intellectual needs are just as important to us as men's are to them and we are not all fulfilled by housework and motherhood alone. For me personally, it was about a greater sense of purpose, leadership and contribution to the world. I knew God had placed more inside of me and I just had not found it yet. And the thought of giving one up, my career, an amazing family life, children, a life of service was aggrieving. I wanted it all and I desperately struggled with the belief that I couldn't have it all. Amongst the stressors of life (my sudden career derailment, the foundation looking as if it was falling apart, being deeply lonely, full of fear from every angle, not trusting myself, and my spiritual guide...) I was turning 30 and I was afraid of what I thought 30 represented. I cried every single day.

Los Angeles Bound

I woke up to the sun peeking into the window onto my face while I was lying on the plush grey leather couch of my friend Tiffany's West Hollywood apartment. I decided to do my morning writing in my journal…what the heck am I doing in Los Angeles, California? I wrote. This is only my third time in California, since most of my career after college was spent in New York City. Tiffany had been listening to my tearful confessions. She was a good friend and wanted to help pull me out of my downward spiral. She called me one day with a one-way ticket from New York to Los Angeles. "Pack a bag and come visit me," she said. I needed to get out of my apartment, out of my head, out of my own overwhelming discouraging beliefs about myself and most things in my life. So I got out of the bed, packed my bags and headed to the west coast. As I laid on the beach for a couple days in the radiant sunshine and the perfect 78-degree weather, I thought about all of my very specific dreams of being a designer in New York City that I had carried so close to my heart since I was a child. I thought about how I set out so long ago to prove every person wrong who didn't think being a fashion designer was a real career. I didn't sleep on the filthy streets on Manhattan to give up now, but I was miserable, confused, and exhausted inside.

I realized in that moment I had locked myself into a narrative and I didn't realize my self-esteem and sense of self was largely connected to that story. The narrative was that I was on my road and I could not deviate when I used to be a person that would create a road where it didn't exist as my friend Danessa would say. I convinced myself of things like, "If I leave NYC and if I don't become the head designer at Gucci...people won't think I'm successful." Things like, "There's no way I can be a creative director of a fashion company and have a successful marriage and family." "Am I smart enough to run a big company?", I questioned myself.

"If I truly step into my power men won't desire me because they will see me as too strong and they desire submission." "Maybe I've been single so long because I'm not lovable or worthy of the love I truly seek." In the past I prided myself on being a very self-aware person that consistently stayed true to my heart, spirit, and gut -- so where is my joy, my peace for being so true to myself? It was like my heart-directed, spiritually-guided GPS had lead me to the wrong place and I didn't know what I wanted anymore, right at the time society was saying "you're 30 and supposed to have it all together". I told myself that I couldn't trust myself, my heart, my gut anymore and all I could do is pull my leopard BCBG sunglasses over my eyes, lay on back on the blue and white striped beach towel and cry.

I prayed, meditated, went to yoga, took a couple of per¬sonal development classes, and even volunteered with an entertainment related women's foundation. I was mad at God, however I need something to inspire me again, give me new direction, or maybe I needed a change of scenery. By the end of my two-week vacation, I was doing

17

freelance design work and decided I was going to pack up my apartment in New York and move to Los Angeles. I didn't know if this was a quarter-life crisis, an "oh my God I'm 30" freak out session or what but I went with it. I moved to Los Angeles in an attempt to break the narrative, my own negative beliefs that were lim¬iting me. Maybe Los Angeles was a more viable city, more conductive for a work/life balance. I mean, I am supposed to be thinking about a family, children and having it all (the way I was moving), just seemed virtually impossible.

One day I received a call from a close friend, Robert, who had also just recently relocated from New York to Los Angles as well. He said "I need your design skills tomorrow." He asked me to drive to Calabasas to the home of a huge international movie star who just happened to be one of my favorite influential people * Richard to do some design consulting for a new clothing line they were developing. I jumped at the opportunity and went for it. The next day I woke up early and drove into the striking hills of this very exclusive community. When I entered the compound I was nervous but excited. I went into the house, introduced myself to the small team in the home theater. I plugged the charger into my MacBook, pulled out my hot pink measuring tape, got clear on the task list, and started working. Before I knew it I was consulting the family on a regular basis. After about a month, I was driving to Calabasas and I had a God moment. I walked into the house and went into the theater but instead of design work the small group watched a home video. Richard and his son had just been skydiving a couple of days prior and he was explaining his personal thoughts and beliefs about fear. How Fear was not real. How fear was a product of our imagination, which usually causes us to misrepresent circumstances in our own minds that may not ever exist. He also explained his experience with fear that day of the expedition. He went moment by moment explaining why fear is a waste of time and energy... It was fascinating. At that moment everything started to seem singularly sur¬real and I knew it was a "God moment".

"What am I doing here?" I thought. Not literally but let's stop and recap this thing… I'm from a small town in Iowa, Waterloo and technically still a resident of New York. I had ever been to California in my life and I decided to pick up and move to this new extremely unfamiliar city. I had been depressed and crying resentful with God for 6 months straight after losing my designer role, I was confused about my future with little self-confidence and full of fear. Here I was standing in the beautiful house of one of the biggest names in Hollywood, not consulting on fashion in this moment but instead having an in-depth conversation about overcoming fear and the power of my own beliefs.

I knew in that moment that God had been working all things together and was using that conversation to speak to me directly. I didn't realize until that moment that I wasn't giving myself the room to grow, to be flexible with God. I had refused to allow my dream to evolve as I was evolving as a woman. The reason why I had been so sad and frustrated with my life was be¬cause I had built these monstrous walls of beliefs that caused me to not only see the world, but mainly myself, from a limited perspective. Faith is a perspective. Somewhere along the way I gained a sense of entitlement with God, like He owed me a reward in exchange for the task list I had completely. I was forgetting that He gave me life! God was right there in my frustration and anger using whomever and whatever it took to speak to me and show me the way I had mentally shifted and started focusing more on all the limitations not the possibilities. All I could see were the things I personally lacked, all that I am not and lost track of everything I am. Brene Brown speaks about how we cannot selectively numb emotions. The thing is when we numb ourselves to being open to hurt, vulnerability, or anything we perceive as a negative emotion, we also numb love, connectivity, creativity and other positive emotions. My fear permeated through every aspect of my life. I started habitually playing small, dulling my own light so people around me wouldn't feel intimidated, being afraid and insecure, all I could think about was TIME. I had so much anxiety about my fleeting time and what I had not accomplished. Did I waste all this time on the wrong path? My biological clock was ticking louder than ever and I didn't have any more time to experiment or be wrong. I had to be absolutely certain or not do it at all. Being consumed with those thoughts literally paralyzed me with fear and I was suffocating. I didn't want to depend on ambiguity of faith or take risks anymore. Though faith and fearlessness had been my reputation, remember "Nerves of Steel". Fortitude and adventure had been the cornerstones of the woman I thought I was. Now I was acting like a terrified little girl and I beat myself up every day for that.

But God…was using one of my lowest, loneliest seasons in my life to shift me into a new direction and one of my favorite influential people Richard to spark up a conversation that I could never forget. A message that spoke directly to my spirit at the perfect time, it spoke to mental prison of self-imposed fear. We sat there and conversed for a while then I excused myself to step outside for a moment to get just some air. It was a bit overwhelming, I was a bit emotional and I couldn't really hold myself together anymore. And in that moment outside it was probably the clearest I've heard God's voice on the beautiful day in the gated compound in the Hidden Hills of Calabasas saying, "Your life is a reflection of the limitations you put on me." I realized that I was my own problem, my perspective had not only been limiting myself but limiting what I would allow God to do in life also.

Afterwards, I decided to head home. I pulled over on my drive and cried one last time about this 30 thing. However, my tears were of repentance and gratitude not regret and confusion. This day wasn't about the celebrity novelty of the situation or even the enlightening conversation. This day was about God showing His faithfulness even in light of my anger. He was showing me how astonishingly mindful He was of every single tear, worry and/or concern. God was proving that He was right there taking every step of the journey with me. That there is no place to low that God won't come and get me. This was a very unexpected highlight in my career and God used that opportunity to say in essence, "Look around, are you impressed? Well even all this is a reflection of your life with limits. Someone, somewhere is depending on you to do what I called you to do, for you to dig out that Greatness in you." God was telling me to think bigger than my own personal career ideas of being a designer of wearable art. I want you to help me change lives and that is how Design+Her+Life was born.

What is Design+Her+Life?

Design+Her+Life is a Chic + purposeful wellness movement that creates environments/products of caring, sharing, and sisterhood conducive for

receiving education, encouragement, and empowerment, specifically for women.

Design+Her+Life INTENTIONS:

Our intentions are to help women like you:

+ Gain a greater sense of self and integrate consistent style + wellness practices into your everyday life.

+ Connect you to a greater sense of purpose, leadership and contribution to the world.

+ Discover the best suited Life+Design™, Support Systems, and your "zone of genius," as it applies to the areas of the business in which you feel you can make the biggest impact.

+ Unlock your inner potential by way of self-reflection, self-acceptance and empowering transformation.

Let's do "Werk"

As I look back on my life, I realized that every time I thought I was being REJECTED from something good...I was being Re-Directed to something BETTER! I was passionate about personal and spiritual development specifically with women along with combining my expertise in the fashion industry. I decided Design+Her+Life would create opportunities for women to see another perspective for the ultimate inside out makeover. I was a spiritual person however, there was a definite disconnect from what I believed God could do and what I believed He would do in my life. I could praise all day in church and pray with thundering certainty for someone else but when it came down to actually executing my purpose and missions I would talk myself right out of the situation. It's my whole-hearted belief, that our greatest struggles are directly connected to our greatest contributions to the world. Before I got too excited about building the movement, I had to acknowledge I was deeply struggling in an area of my life and thought life, I had to be willing to do my own personal development "werk" first.

Women Community Power

I didn't realize the power of a women's community until I joined a couple and I knew Design+Her+Life had to have community elements centered around our identities as women. I needed a break from only attending my old church, all the submission talk and cliquey church culture, "you have to be married to attend our event or be in this clique" was starting to really take a toll on me; I was tired of the inclusion/exclusion based on my marital status. However, I still thought attending church was an important aspect of my spiritual practices. Church for me is inspiring, an opportunity to hear greats like Bishop TD Jakes bring the Bible to life is powerful but still just one community amongst others like community-based service, fellowship with liked-minded people, meditation, journaling and accountability group. Who is going to help you consistently execute what you learned in church? When I think of my spirit it's not just through religious lenses, it's through an overall well-being lens. I knew I needed a set of spiritual practices to nourish my spirit consistently. So I joined a personal development women's community (collective learning environment) that opened me up to a whole new set of perspectives. A collec¬tive learning environment brings people together for sharing, learning, and discovery. Within a community all participants take respon¬sibility for achieving the learning objectives lead by a coach/facilitator. This particular community was structured with an actual program of 20 diverse, amazing women who invested in the program for a set number of weeks. More than anything this structure and commitment helped me become more aware of my narratives, limiting prospective, flush out some of the fear, and get expressively clear about my intentions for the direction of my life and what I wanted to accomplish with my time in the program. This structured, yet free flow environment, created a consistent 'Space' in my busy life to devote energy to work on myself. Every day, I had a morning practice and every week I was doing homework. Author Alan Fine notes in his book, You Already Know How to be Great, "Performance is not always about information acquisition as much as it is information application."

Oftentimes we know what to do we just don't implement it consistently enough to maintain the positives change in our lives. My groups of women were there to help hold me accountable to the previously set intentions long enough to create better habits.

The group also helped me with executing on the information I acknowledged as truth but wasn't practicing consistently. Finally, being in women's communities throughout the years has taught me how to be more gentle on myself in the course correction process. Hearing women tell their stories similar to what we are doing with this book let me know I'm not alone in my feelings, fears, or life shifts. As a result of these experiences I was able to see I had been my own worst enemy, inflexible, mean and unforgiving with myself during this ever-changing, universal human growth process called life.

Limiting Beliefs

(about ourselves, what's possible, and God)

To make sure we are on the same page, when referring to "beliefs system", we are using the definition of beliefs as follows: beliefs are deeply rooted convictions about the world and about ourselves. This could refer to religious views, as we often choose our religion to help frame the way we see the world. However, this is not limited to religion and it doesn't have to be the only influencer in the context of this book. It's the paradigm, the lenses, the prospective, and way you see the world. Often times our belief systems are shaped by our experiences and how we have been conditioned to have certain dispositions toward one thing or another. The challenge is that most of our beliefs are generalizations about our past, based on our interpretations of our experiences. Most of us do not consciously decide or recognize moment-to-moment how our deeply rooted beliefs influence our actions. Sadly, many of us are on autopilot. It's difficult to recognize our story/prospective is only a single story, which is one aspect of the truth. Just because our thoughts are familiar and comfortable doesn't mean those thoughts are serving the best version of you or creating a desired result. "The single story creates stereo¬types, and the problem with stereotypes is not that they are untrue, but that they are incomplete. They make one story become the only story," says Chimamanda Ngozi Adichie in her 2009 TED Global Talk. Bishop TD Jakes also posed an insightful question to the congregation one day I was visiting The Potter's House church. He said, "I want each of you to challenge our absolutes. Because you could be absolutely wrong. You could be crucifying someone with a truth or perception that is skewed by a limited prospective!" I love that!!I couldn't understand why I struggled so much with the belief that I just wasn't enough and/or worthy. My single story, perception and beliefs had been skewed by a limited prospective of myself. I was comparing myself to a standard of greatness I was being defined by cultural influence, friends, family, instead of defining my greatness for myself. I had adopted the bad habit of not stopping to celebrate my own milestones, glimpse of greatness along the way forgetting that our journey of growth is nourished by encouragement. I definitely picked this up from living in a city like New York where the daily pace can be energizing at times but often times unforgiving… "Move or get out of the way".

So let's take a moment to illustrate how our personal thoughts are directly connected to our personal action. I had a belief that I wasn't worthy of the love I sought. And let's use media messages as an example, many that suggest most of American women don't have the right body type for a man to be happy (only Victoria Secret models get great men right? Lol). Now let's use environmental influence, where many old women I spoke with said, "every man cheats" or "all men think about is sex." Well after we see and hear these messages over and over, we start to become influenced by the messages. Come on Ladies let's be honest. We secretly and sometimes unconsciously place that message in a mental folder that can either create a belief or reinforce a belief you already associate with yourself. Before long I was self-sabotaging every relationship, secretly I'm believing I'm not enough for a man not to cheat or that I need an attribute I don't currently have to keep this man in love with me or all he wants is sex anyway. So as opposed to being disappointed and heart-broken in the end, I made a decision about my intentions and actions before I ever started the interaction. I just won't give 100% or get fully connected or allow myself to fall deeply in love. As a result, I failed to experience authentic connections and then I am wondering why I am so lonely for real connection. This is just one example. However, what I'm finding in my sessions is that many people are walking around secretly thinking were not enough, not smart enough, not wealthy enough, whatever...men and women alike. As a result of these types of beliefs we overcompensate, we see men spend obscene amounts of money on cars and women, women are baring it all on social media outlets. These are just a few examples of using momentary attention to satisfy a thirst for a heightened sense of worthiness. The belief that "I am not enough" or any limiting belief creates actions that limits us from experiencing true connections and showing up in the world authentically.

"Sow a thought and you reap an action;

sow an act and you reap a habit;

sow a habit and you reap a character;

sow a character and you reap a destiny."

-Ralph Waldo Emerson

I am now consistently training myself and the women I work with to explore two questions when we feel ourselves getting stuck in limiting or negative beliefs.

#1 Am I willing to discover/accept a prospective outside of your own? (One that serves me and my overall intention)

#2 Have I retreated into a story that is not serving me?

When you become the center of the criticism and not the action/behavior it's a clear indication you have retreated into the story. The difference is the context of how you tell the story: "Owning our story can be hard but not nearly as difficult as spending our lives running from it. Embracing our vulnerabilities is risky but not nearly as dangerous as giving up on love, belonging and joy—the experiences that make us the most vulnerable. Only when we are brave enough to explore the darkness will we discover the infinite power of our light." – Brene Brown. My story was keeping me from seeing what God could do in my life that may not be comfortable but necessary to get me where I desire to be with my career, family and greatness. Often times we are limited, not because our dreams and visions are impossible, but by our limited perceptions of what is possible. Many of us don't have real life roadmaps of how to make what we've dreamed possible, so we stop believing it possible and we stop trusting that it was God who gave it to us! That's a limiting belief. I can't do it…, I'm too old…, I'm not worthy of…, This will never work…, all these are limiting beliefs. Hebrews 11:6 says "But without faith it is impossible to please him: for he that cometh to God must believe that He IS, and that He is a rewarder of them that diligently seek him." This scripture is a reflection of how beliefs are essential to results in every area of our lives. You must first believe that God exists before anything else can follow, the same applies to our lives. We must first believe that IT exists, it's truly possibly before it can reach fruition. It sounds simple right, but it's the first step to any and every result you desire in your life; the step we often overlook and usually struggle the most with. When I talk about doing the werk it is first identifying what your limiting beliefs are and how are you perpetuating your limits by how you tell your story/belief to yourself and others. Beliefs are directly connected to actions. Our lives unfold to reflect our beliefs…our personal truths, change my beliefs, change my life.

Let's be real, change is hard! Change doesn't just happen by being inspired. It's forcefully imposing your will on your comfort zone, daily. Changes when it comes to personal development work is extremely hard right, it's the real work, and it's confronting and draining. You're not memorizing random words or workout exercises or reading about this extraneous subject…it's about YOU. Don't think of yourself as weak if you can't do this alone because sometimes you're dealing with your layers of yourself, discovering connections to your bad behavior and evaluating your upbringing. That's why it's encouraging to get a therapist or coach to help with the heavy mental lifting. You are often times resurfacing the pieces of yourself that you would rather leave buried, but left unresolved these pieces could be stopping you from showing up in the world as powerfully and as authentically as God created you to be. Change is not just hard for you, it's hard for everyone. According to the American Psychological Association here are a few tips we can do to create more lasting, positive lifestyle and behavior changes:

1. Start small.

Don't try to do too much too fast. Identify realistic short-term and long-term goals, break down your goals into small, manageable steps that are specifically defined and can be measured.

2. Change one behavior at a time.

Unhealthy behaviors develop over the course of time, so replacing unhealthy behaviors with healthy ones requires time. Many people run into problems when they try to change too much too fast. As new healthy behaviors become a habit, try to add another goal that works toward the overall change you're striving for.

3. Accountability.

Talk to others about what you are doing. Consider joining a women's community or support group. Having someone with whom to share your struggles and successes makes the work easier and the mission less intimidating.

With the ladies in our Design+Her+Life "Werkrooms" we start with this ID (personal identification) exercise. Let's do "Werk"!

Step #1: Find a quiet place and use the wheel to rate your level of satisfaction with each area of your life. Here are some example questions to help you get started.

We start with Self/Spirit as it is at the core of everything else!

Self/Spirit: Think about your personal & spiritual well-being How often do you engage in events and/or activities that address your personal and spiritual development? Are you struggling with Fear, Self-Doubt, Forgiveness or Self-Acceptance? Are you trying new experiences and/or seeking to learn on a regular basis? How connected do you feel with your spirit? Are you satisfied with your relationship with your spiritual side? How connected do you feel with God? Do you have spiritual practices to help grow your spirituality? Do you respect and love yourself? Do you love yourself?

Work: Think about your business, career goals, current position, etc. Is your career where you want it to be? Are you happy with your work? Do you feel like you're giving 100% to your work? Are you valued at work? Is your work satisfying to you?

Wealth: Think saving, future money planning, salary & investments. Are you earning enough income to satisfy your current needs? Are you financially setup for future growth in wealth?

Social: Think friendships, entertainment, hobbies & travel. Do you have enjoyable activities/hobbies in your life? Do you travel? Are you adventurous and try new things regularly? Are you spending time with friends? Are you enjoying your life and expanding socially? Are you satisfied with the level of
activity that you do?

Purpose: Think about your life's work,
contribution and how to use your gifts to serve the world. Are you using your gifts to serve the world in any way? What is your contribution to society and people in your life? Have you defined your own definition of success?

-Give Back: Think about giving to the less fortunate, donations & service work? Do you think service is important? What in your life helps you develop a greater sense of social responsibility? What do you do to expose yourself to diversity and multiculturalism? How do you gain awareness to social causes?

Health: Think fitness, diet, overall wellness & body image. Do you feel good about your health? Do you feel good about your body? Are you satisfied with your level of fitness? Have you done any research lately about new dietary or fitness practices?

Love: Think relationship, marriage, dating, and life partner. Do you feel loved? Do you know your love language? Do you feel connected in your relationship? Do you feel worthy of the love you desire? How often are you expressing love to others? Are you satisfied with your love life?

Family: Think parents, grandparents, children, family lineage, and family reunions. Do you have a positive relationship with your family? Do you feel supported by your family? Do you feel your family supports you? Are you aware of your family history?

Step #2: See Wheel Image

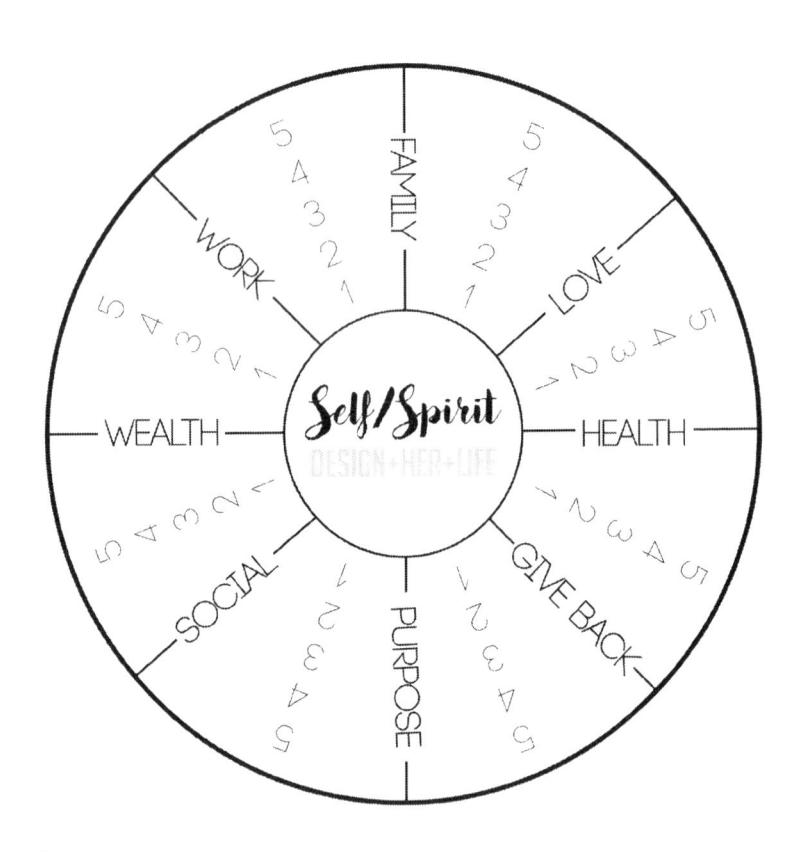

Step #3: After taking time to honestly reflect on your personal level of satisfaction with the areas of importance in your life. Decide only (1-2) areas you are committed to working on. Remember to start with small and intentional steps to build momentum to move your life forward. It's about advancing, challenging yourself and creating a lasting change in your life.

Step #4 Create a timeframe: Without a specific time frame tied to your goals there's no sense of urgency. However if you anchor this goal within a timeframe, then you've set your unconscious mind into motion to begin working on the goal.

Step #5 Identify any Limiting Beliefs you might have about your success in this area: Define what success could look like to you, do you really believe it's possible? Why or Why not?

Step #6 Set Goals with Intention: Being Intentional just simply means that we choose to act deliberately, purposefully, and consciously. Choose a few manageable steps that are specifically defined and can be measured.

Step #7 Accountability: Remember we often time know we already possess the knowledge to get the results we want in our lives, we may just lack the discipline, motivation or belief that we can do it long enough to see the desired results. Ask for support!

Step #8 Write Progress: If you're a person that keeps a consistent journal, write about your progress. If not you can find a Jar and write a small note every single time you make progress. The purpose is to have a place to go if you get discouraged at any point. Accomplishing small goals gives your brain a nice, refreshing spritz of dopamine that acts as motivation to keep going. This will help you remind yourself you are indeed making an assertive effort to make positive change in your life.

Step #9 Celebrate You: The behavior we celebrate are behaviors we will repeat. Don't celebrate so much you lose focus and progress.

Step #10 Repeat Steps 4-9 for an (1) additional area of improvement

Doing the "werk" to get to a place of true self-acceptance and self-love is not about being self-centered or weak. It means that you accept the responsibility for your own development, growth and happiness.

One of my greatest inspirations for the personal and spiritual developmental efforts I continue to make (include Therapy) is not to change all of my core values or essence of who I. I am looking to constantly refine to a better version of myself and like the Bible describes as being transformed into the likeness of God that is, glory to glory. It is my belief now that no matter how it looks on social media, TV or the outside looking in, No one has it all together. Life will not stop forcing us to change but we can choose how we grow with the inevitable change. I want to operate from a place of power and worthiness not living my life on autopilot habitually operating out or fear, pain and rigid beliefs that limit me from seeing what's really possible. I wish the same for you. Be courageous enough to do the "Werk"!

Passion Prayer Purpose...A Collection of Stories to Help Any Woman Design+Her+Life.

This is a collection of young powerful women who have submitted stories from all over the country. We have come together to recount our stories of obstacles + triumphs. With the overarching themes:

Passion, the work that deeply drives us to greatness + how you can find that unique Life+Design™ for yourself!

Prayer, a diverse look at the importance of having a great spiritual foundation!

Purpose, how our greatest struggles are directly connected to our greatest contributions to the world.

From entrepreneurs to working mothers, this book is sure to be entertaining + inspirational with amazing practical advice. My hope is that women will use this book as a tool to help fully accept and love their authentic selves and their journeys. I want women to realize the life-shaping power of how we tell are stories can make us victims or victors. When women take the positions of victors we are able to connect our own stories and experiences to a powerful, tangible contribution to the world.

Nicole Sallis
Creator of Design+Her+ Life, Fashion Expert, Author, Educator, Motivator, Chic+Purposeful…. More than Just Fashion

With more than 10 years of extensive corporate and entrepreneurial experience in the fashion industry, Nicole's expertise includes creative design, fashion forecasting, product development, visual merchandising, branding, styling and producing fashion shows.

She has worked with numerous celebrities, creative brands and television networks in both the New York City and Los Angeles markets. Nicole has consulted with luxury brands such as Estee-Lauder and Neiman Marcus as well as television networks such as BET, VH1 and MTV. She's developed innovative products for Macys, Kohl's, Hanesbrands, Forever 21, the NBA and has provided image consulting to Russell Simmons, The Smiths, Nicki Minaj, Nelly and many more. Outside of the fashion industry, Nicole focuses her free time on connecting service, creativity, education and empowering young people and women. She currently serves as the Program Director of STEM for the Arts Urban Outreach Initiatives for girls. Nicole has created curriculum for creative writing, leadership, fashion and creative empowerment programs and workshops for numerous universities and organizations like Harlem Children Zone.

She is a published author and poet inspiring audiences as a powerful speaker, influential panelist, trained facilitator and event host at universities and conferences across the country. Nicole has spoken to large crowds at venues such as the world renowned Madison Square Garden and has also been the Executive Producer for the Dress for Success Fashion Experience for National Society of Black Engineers National Conference.

Nicole is a Christian and published her first book Words Transform, in 2011, which sold over 3,000 copies. In 2015, she founded Design+Her+Life LLC— an organization that promotes women's empowerment, style, wellness and spirituality. Nicole created a series of retreats and werkrooms-focuses on motivating women—young and old— to fully Connect to a greater sense of purpose, leadership and contribution to the world.

Nicole is a graduate of Iowa State University and has a Bachelor of Science degree in Business with a specialization in Apparel Design, Merchandising and Production. She resides and maintains an office in the New York City area.

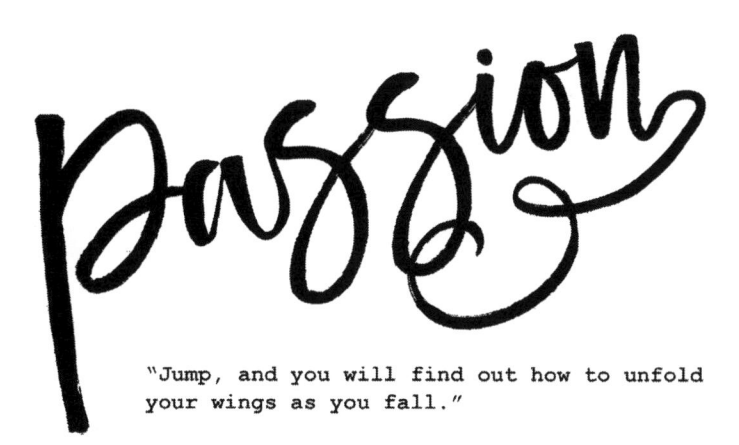

passion

"Jump, and you will find out how to unfold your wings as you fall."

-Ray Bradbury

Keep your head up, Keep your heart strong

     I can stop it all right now. I can make all the pain go away. I have the power to end this. My tomorrow will be no more. I cried and prayed and cried some more. Here I am such a talented, positive soul sitting on the bed in my boyfriend's guest bedroom, in the dark, with 40 plus Percocet's in my hand. The pills were from my hand surgery several months back. In my mind I knew I couldn't or wouldn't take the pills but the mere fact that I'm holding them in my hands and toying with the idea of taking them is enough. An hour or so has passed but feels more like 10 hours. God, please help me through this, things can't possibly get any worse than this. I'm not crazy, only crazy people have these thoughts! What will my family think of me if I end my life? What will those who I speak life into feel about me taking my life? Although, when I look back on this day I see it as just another bad day, I know the severity of the heartache I could have caused. The severity of the heartache I've felt. I've become the strongest I've ever been after that dreadful night. I made a promise to myself that I would never allow anything or anyone to ever make me feel that low to believe that my life wasn't worth living. God will never put more on us than we can bear. Speak life into every situation whether good or not so good and even if it seems like a dead end. Believe in yourself even if no one else will. I don't regret that experience and I don't mind telling it. We are all human and will fall short on God's words at times but it is important that we get up no matter what! If you get knocked down 9 times dust yourself off and get ready for round 10. I pray that my words touch the heart of someone and help you to understand that your life is worth living.

February 21, 2013

     Exhausted, I've had about 9 hours of sleep in the past 3 days and have yet to eat at all today. Sadly, this has become my normal these days. On the Megabus, on my way back to NYC from doing an event in Maryland and all I can think about is getting home to sew this dress. As the bus pulls into the parking lot I gather my belongings in a frenzy to hurry off the bus. I grab my suitcase from the bottom of the bus which has to weigh about 65 pounds and stands tall to my chest. I begin to run as quickly as possible from fabric store to fabric store in search of the desired fabric to make the dress. Not only do I have to start and finish this dress tonight; I have to overnight ship it so that my client can have it the next day for her grandmother's funeral. Pushing through my dizziness and fatigue I finally find what I am looking for. I try my hardest to make it to the train; my mind says just keep going, keep walking, you got this! Meanwhile, my body is saying the complete opposite. When I realize I can't make it to the train I began to hail down a taxi cab. Good luck catching a cab during rush hour in Times Square I said to myself under my breath. A very pleasant man with an English accent noticed that I wasn't feeling well and asked if I needed his assistance. I replied yes and he began to help me. Minutes later, we finally managed to get a cab.

As I attempted to take a step to enter the cab I felt like I was losing control of my body and everything went black. I fell back into (who I think was the man who helped me) arms. I could hear people screaming from every direction. "Don't put her in that cab", yelled one woman. "Is she a diabetic", "is she drunk", call 911. It felt like a movie. I didn't know whether to feel embarrassed because I passed out in Times Square in front of hundreds of people or afraid because I felt like my life was ending. Honestly, I felt a little of both. In my mind, I thought,

"This is it! This is how my life will end, this is my story! I have so much more I want to accomplish. I don't want to die." When I came to, I was surrounded by worried and caring people.

You may be surprised how people come together to help those in need in a time of a crisis. One man poured his juice in my mouth, a woman fed me some homemade rice pudding and another woman called my mom to let her know what was happening. These people waited with me and held my hand until paramedics arrived. I explained to the paramedics that I didn't eat all day, had been working a full time job, and running what was becoming a full time business. Not to mention, I didn't have any proper rest in months. I was exhausted; my body had reached its breaking point. I refused to go to the hospital to get checked because I knew it would take time away from me making the dress. One of the medics advised that if I don't take care of myself that I won't be around to make dresses. I gave him a smile and slight nod as I signed the papers to be released from the ambulance. I promised him that I would eat and take better care of myself and then made my way out. Looking back, I don't know if I was foolish or just plain ole passionate about designing. The moment I entered the cab I instantly regretted not going to the hospital but it still didn't deter me from my main agenda which was to go home and make the dress. I began to make the dress when I arrived home but was too sick, tired, and flustered to continue, so I prepared my resignation letter instead.

Feb 22, 2013

To xxxx,

Thank you for the opportunity to be a part of such a great company....

As I began to put my resignation letter together I started to ask myself am I really going to hand this in? Am I ready for what's to come? How will I support myself financially if this doesn't work? What if people don't like my clothing? What if no one supports me? What is my plan? Do I even have a plan? What happens if I fail? Maybe I should stay.... After trying to negatively talk myself out of following my dreams as we sometimes do, I finished my resignation letter and handed it in the next day. I was proud of myself for doing what so many are afraid to do.

"There is freedom waiting for you on the breezes of the sky. And you ask 'What if I fall?' Oh but my darling what if you fly?"
                                             -Erin Hanson

One of the hardest decisions I've ever had to make was to question popular thinking and take a leap of faith on my God given talents. I had no idea where I would end up or if people would even support my business. What I did know was that I had a gift. I knew I could make people feel good by making them look good. I knew my level of creativity would take me places that my "job" couldn't. I knew if I would only jump that eventually my parachute would open. How could God give me such a gift and allow me to fail? The thought of it was absurd. I had to jump.

Two weeks later…

I decided to visit a close girlfriend of mine in Philadelphia for the weekend to celebrate this new found freedom and also get my thoughts together. I thought this trip was exactly what I needed before I began this new journey of entrepreneurship. Monday came and I began to reflect; today marks the first day of the rest of my life. As I let that settle in, my heart began to pound rapidly and my breaths shorter than the one before. I was having a mild panic attack. "What in the world did I just do?" The more I tried to calm my nerves the more I panicked, but I knew there was no turning back now. Today will mark the beginning of the rest of my life. It's time to say yes to living!

"Entrepreneurship is living a few years of your life like most people won't, so that you can spend

the rest of your life like most people can't."

Looking back on things, I think the hardest part may have been to actually make the decision to follow my heart. I want you to ask yourself; what would you do if you weren't afraid and knew you couldn't fail? Now, I want you to go out and do it! A lot of us live by the myth that we have time to do just about everything so we tend to put things off until we feel everything is in order. In all actuality we don't have time. All we have is right now and what perfect time to live the life you desire than now?! What if I tell you that failure doesn't exist? Would you believe that to be true? For example, if you were to lose your job without warning you'd probably look at it as some form of failure and/or as a negative. Now, what happens if you begin to stretch your thinking in ways that you never would have had you not been fired. You then use being fired as an opportunity to go after your dreams which can be to go back to school, start your own business, learn something new etc. This now puts you in a position to grow and be even better than you were before you were fired. Would you still consider being fired failing? Probably not. You have to realize what opportunities are right in front of you and use them in your own best interest. You also have to choose to see the positive in every negative and choose to be your very best. Not every situation that appears to be negative actually is.

"Take advantage of the opportunity of a lifetime in the lifetime of the

opportunity".

I've lost count on the number of tears I've cried, the amount of times I've asked myself what possessed me to do this and definitely the amount of times I wanted to give up. I never thought it would be this hard but like my mentor and one of the best motivational speakers Dr. Eric Thomas always say "If it was easy then everybody would do it". No one said it would be easy but it will definitely be worth it! The one percent didn't make it to the top from going down an easy road. The recipe for success is putting consistent hard work, period. I put blood, sweat, tears and maybe a few other things into my business and I wouldn't trade my process. I'm the strongest I've ever been and I know I could never be half the woman I am today had I taken the elevator up. My faith has been tested and my patience tried, but God! When you begin to walk out on faith and follow your dreams be prepared to be called crazy. Be prepared to lose some friends in the process of you following your dreams. Be prepared to walk down some lonely roads, prepare yourself to be misunderstood but don't give up! Be willing to put 120% effort 24/7 on what you believe in or give nothing at all. Whether your dream is to become an entrepreneur or desire to work for the company of your dreams first you must believe that you deserve it then go out and fight for it! Be sure to have patience and faith even when things don't seem to be going your way. You have to believe that you can do whatever you put your mind to because everything around you at some point or another will try to show you that you can't. Persevere, fail forward, create, and never stop believing in your dreams. Never settle!

"In order to succeed, we must first believe that we can." -Nikos Kazantzakis

I absolutely love what I do. I can't thank God enough for not only allowing me to know what my passion is but giving me the strength to follow it. I have a great support system of family and friends. I enjoy meeting new clients and creating amazing clothing for them. When I think back to when I began this journey 3 years ago I never imagined becoming so enlightened on this path. I've learned so much about myself and the world in itself. I began to meditate some years back which is one of the best things I could have done for myself. I advise everyone to do it. I've never felt more alive and appreciative in my life as I do now. I know for a fact that this is due to my journey as an entrepreneur. What started out as wanting to become a Fashion Designer has escalated to what can I do with my life that will not only add value to the world we live in but touch the hearts and minds of many. I love to pour positivity into people; to hear someone say because of you I've followed my dreams is something bigger than material things. Being a cheerful giver is one of the best things you can do for yourself and others. Give love, give a smile, give hugs, give a prayer and enjoy doing it. Aspire to inspire!

Develop success from failures. Discouragement and failure are two of the surest stepping stones to success. -Dale Carnegie

Of course being an entrepreneur comes with a lot of highs but there are many mental lows. Mental lows are more common than one may think. I have no plan. Every designer seems to have everything in order so why am I struggling? Why can't I seem to get any help? Why did God choose me to walk this path? I want to give up! This isn't fair. Some people will never understand the sacrifices I've made to get here and to reach a certain level of success. Why am I not receiving the support I feel I deserve? My relationship is in shambles, I barely speak to my friends, I don't go out anymore because I really have to budget my money right. I no longer have the luxury of receiving a paycheck every week. My credit is the worst it's ever been, my student loans are past due and they've threatened to put them in collection. I'm so stressed; I'm sad and angry at times. I scream inside as the tears flow down my face. I don't want this struggle. I just want a successful business! Why is this so hard?! I'm so lonely. Everything around me is so dark, no matter how much light is around me!

"If you want a thing bad enough then go out and fight for it. Work day and night for it. Give up your time and your peace and your sleep for it."
-The Optimist Creed

Most people want the success but few people are willing to put in the work to achieve it. The road to success isn't an easy one, it will be rocky, some peaks and valleys. You may fail at something but understand there is growth in "failure". You have to find balance in your failures and successes. Be sure to surround yourself with positive people. Be careful of who and what you allow your energy to and the energy you allow into your life. Surround yourself with doers, people who think like you, who will motivate you and who will take you out of your comfort zone. In case you don't know, there is no growth in comfort zones. Have you ever heard the saying 'if you're the smartest person in the room then you might be in the wrong room?" If this is you then it might be time to change your circle. Success requires patience; it requires leadership and great thinking skills. Be open to learning something new every day and apply what you've learned to your life. Make a conscious effort to be the best you every single day of your life. I challenge you to go after whatever it is you're passionate about and if you don't have an idea of what that is, make it a priority to figure it out. You owe it to yourself to live your absolute best life. I believe in you.

Promise yourself...

"To be so strong that nothing can disturb your peace of mind. To talk health, happiness and prosperity to every person you meet. To make all your friends feel that there is something in them. To look at the sunny side of everything and make your optimism come true. To think only of the best, to work only for the best, and to expect only the best. To be just as enthusiastic about the success of others as you are about your

own. To forget the mistakes of the past and press on to the greater achievements of the future. To wear a cheerful countenance at all times and give every living creature you meet a smile. To give so much time to the improvement of yourself that you have no time to criticize others. To be too large for worry, too noble for anger, too strong for fear, and too happy to permit the presence of trouble."

Fashion Designer Zina Lanay Walcott, is the now the CEO and creative director of Zina Lanay and Ze Elle by Zina Lanay. Her business continues to grow and she is more than ecstatic for what the future holds. She continues to work hard; focusing on the present and future of her business and will continue to live her dream.

Entrepreneurship

I don't really remember anyone ever speaking to me about careers until my senior year. It might have been briefly mentioned during my sophomore year in high school but other than that no prior preparation for college or the real world. The lack of apprenticeship programs is a problem our youth are facing today. However, I saw both parents working every day, grandparents worked, and anyone who wasn't working was in school. Although my youngest aunt was more of a free bird, I saw her take chances and live life freely! She went to cosmetology school and opened a hair salon in an area that was booming at the time. As I watched her, I admired the freedom she had. She did things her way and was unapologetic, and that takes courage and gusts. Of course as I got older I learned that even with freedom there has to be a plan in place to get you to the next level. I've always been told the three keys to success are preparation, preparation and preparation, and if you don't plan, you plan to fail, is true.

I've always had a love for film and TV. But it wasn't until high school when I took a TV production class that I really became enamored in that world. I enjoyed learning the behind the scenes business and creative process. That love and curiosity carried on to college where I studied electronic media and PR (Public Relations) and minored in theatre.

Fast forward, my first interview was with ABC Phoenix, and needless to say I was extremely excited. I went in for the interview and the head of the department talked with me for a while. I did not get the position but I do remember him asking me what I really wanted to do. That made me realize that I didn't have a plan or any set goals for myself. I left the office feeling excited yet uncertain in how to figure out what I really wanted to do. In the meantime, I landed a position with a university in the admission's department. I was excited for a few reasons. The obvious one of course was steady income, secondly, it was something I was familiar with, and third, I was starting my professional work career. I primarily took this job because I needed to make a living and the pay was good for fresh out of college. Once I decided I was going to take the position I then thought about ways I could use this experience as a stepping stone to something later. I quickly soared and became a top performer in my department, receiving recognition and awards. I was in this sales position for six years before I switch to the marketing department.

This was my first job in corporate and it taught me a couple of things. The first thing is that you are replaceable, this is important to remember! Second, in order to get a real piece of the pie or make some real money, you either have to dedicate your life to the job or have something invaluable to offer and even then you are still replaceable. Lastly you have no real friends in business because it's just that: business.

During my time at the university I started my own event planning business, Epiphany Events, LLC. I went into event planning because it was something I've done in the past and enjoyed it. Also during that time, I moved into the marketing department. I had begun to plan bigger events, so I was getting a lot of experience. I started the business with a partner. He was a former basketball player, who had so many connections in the sports world, which quickly lead into the entertainment circle. Epiphany events was my first business endeavor. Even though I had no real plan outside of making money, I was young and eager and took the leap.

Epiphany Events was a premiere event planning business. We did everything from nonprofit fundraisers, fashion shows, weekly promo-tion nights at the night club, to bigger annual events, like Super Bowl, Nascar, Kentucky Derby and so on. I'm sure this all sounds great but when starting your own business, you also have to be able to fund it. There were things I didn't know. First, when starting a business have a budget or know how you plan to fund it. Secondly, have short term goals and objectives. Last, but not least, have some cushion money put away. I don't think I could say that there is a particular amount but it has to be something that you're comfortable with. Like most new business owners, I was still working my day job. There is a list of things that come up on the day to day, let alone the budgets for the actual events. So remember, if you are planning to jump all in, just be prepared!

Although I had never owned a business before and neither had my partner, I knew what experience I had from sales, marketing and leadership roles. I felt confident in my people skills and relationship building skills. However, I was not sure about all the paperwork and procedures, but what I didn't know, Google did!

The first big event was at the W Hotel in Scottsdale, Arizona. Epiphany Events partnered with another entertainment company to host the event. Epiphany brought in a charitable organization, produced a fashion show, and gave a percentage of the proceeds to the charity. Here's where the lesson begins. First, contracts are very important. Second, there must be clarity of roles, pay and contribution. Finally, there are no friends in business, it's business first. After a few bad business breakups and former contractors who tried to sue us, I was quickly learning. I needed to become more business savvy. I needed to make sure everything was in writing and I needed to follow my gut.

Moving to Arizona taught me about survival. I also learned a much harder lesson and that is a job does not guarantee stability. It does not mean you will be completely comfortable either. However, what it does guarantee is you spending a significant amount of your life's time working and building someone else's vision.

Shortly after coming back from maternity leave I was fired from my job. I saw it coming, there had been cuts and reorganization within my department and the company. There were a lot of underpaid, unhappy employees. It was no surprise but I was still shocked. In a way I wanted to be freed from the repetitive routine but when it actually happened I felt unsure. It was like a caged bird set free, but forgot how to fly. I had kids now, it was not just me anymore and that made me more nervous. At that point the business had slowed down, I had twins and shit load of bills.

At this point a decision had to be made on the next steps to take. My partner always thought big no matter what the situation was in front of us. There was a part of me that agreed with him but the mother in me couldn't see past what was in front of me right now. I didn't know what was next which was ok when it was just me. It wasn't ok now that I had these two precious babies to care for. So we decided to split up in terms of our functionality of the business. I moved back to Chicago temporarily for more support with the kids. My partner continued to travel and promote the company.

I'm originally from Chicago but had not been living in Chicago since I graduated high school. I was away for almost 10 years. Needless to say it was a hard adjustment, my life that I created for myself was gone. I became a recluse for a while. I never had the time to readjust, because the changes all just happened so fast. I went from working a job, having a thriving business, traveling, and kids to constantly having my parents tell me what they thought I should be doing. That was extremely difficult for me and I felt trapped.

The blessing in all the chaos was my time was free. I realized that I didn't want just a job anymore, because it would just occupy my time away from my kids. I didn't realize just how much time my kids would consume. As I've mentioned, I have twin boys and the younger twin, Noah, had some unforeseen medical issues. His hearing had been impaired for the first year of his life and was diagnosed with a developmental delay. I would wonder why he was always so quiet; my baby couldn't hear clearly. I mean I can laugh one hundred percent now because I put in the work. All the doctor appointments, therapy sessions, surgery, evaluations and more therapy. It is a great deal of work and extremely time consuming. I couldn't imagine having to take off days constantly or leave early. I remember I used to listen to my girlfriend rant about how the employer always had something to say about her calling off or needing time, but at the end of the day, she had to do what she had too.

In all honesty it's been a blessing in disguise. It takes a high level energy every day to be present with your kids and really be emotionally available. It takes a lot of energy out of you when working a job for eight hours for an employer that's not flexible and you don't want to be there. Sometimes things happen because they are a part of your journey and are working for the greater good. I now know just how valuable my time is and if I'm not doing something I love, I want to enjoy it raising my sons.

During my time settling into this new life as a mom, my business partner continued on with the business. Epiphany Events has now evolved into the OA Agency, www.oaagency.com which is celebrity talent acquisitions for corporate, brands, venues, and promoters, and international event facilitators for concerts, tour and special events. I was extremely proud of the successes but my heart wasn't in it. It was time for me to rediscover what I wanted to do in alignment with my priorities.

It took some time for me to rediscover who I was. I started to pay attention to my likes and dislikes. I kept my circle small. I spent time with myself, getting to know the person I had become. I worked a few odd projects here and there. I would pray that I would be surrounded by like-minded individuals. Individuals who had similar interest and goals. I would ask for direction in my journey. Then one day, talking to a very close friend, he asked me what I was passionate about? What did I love so much that I would do it for free? The only thing that came to mind was TV and film but I didn't know in what capacity.

During that time, I really got hooked on social media. Social media was my outlet, my eyes and ears to the outside world. I watched everyday girls build and grow their brand. It took some patience and consistency but I saw steady growth. I watched high profile individuals and companies use the platform as a vehicle to build their distinct brands and capitalize on it. The natural hair community is a perfect example of how these hair care lines have reached out to natural hair girls and if they have a big enough following, companies are bringing them on as the brand ambassador for that product line. This was ingenious to me, easy free marketing! It peeked my interest to understand more and how to apply my skills.

I made the decision to start Twinn Media Group, LLC, www.twinnmediagroup.com. TMG's mission is to continue to build your brand through creative content generation and an increased online presence. We will use social media to develop genuine relationships with the consumers and local businesses by developing an online trust that will translate to offline interactions. We will turn your social media platforms into communities where people talk and engage with your company, product or brand, ultimately turning those lookers into customers and existing clientele into a walking advertisement.

Shortly after I started working on TMG, I still felt disconnected. I was working on two accounts but I still felt like there is more that I wanted to do. Being a business owner was just a part of it and I knew this business would tie into whatever else I did. So I began looking into schooling, mostly graduate school. I had started graduate school back in Arizona. I had tossed around the idea before of going back to school but during the process things were always being held up. Well by chance I came across a Tribeca film school ad on Facebook so I took the chance and clicked. The process was swift and almost too smooth. But that's when I knew that this is what I should be doing. Only this time around the goal was to refresh my skills and make some connections within the film industry.

Five years ago I would not have imagined the journey I've been on. However, I am grateful for all the lessons and experiences because that continues to shape and mold me every day. I will be graduating in October 2016 with a degree in film. I have been fortunate enough to work on a few feature films and will have produced three short films by the end of this year. Even in this business it's still a grind because I am still my own boss. So the entrepreneur spirit still reigns true. The key to lasting in this business is patience, persistence and consistency.

I'm sure your wondering what happened to TMG, the social media company. Well it actually has become very useful. I had attended a great networking event that allowed filmmakers to view their trailers and seek help. Some of the films were being released and just promoting and some were in pre-production and needed crew and funding. The one thing all the filmmakers in the room said was that they needed help with the social media and that they lacked a social media presence. Of course this was music to my ears. See sometimes we get prepared for things we don't even know about. But I felt prepared and ready to confidently work the room. I was able to take something that I liked doing and link it in with what I love doing and that's making films.

I've been able to restart my life twice now. I have a new business that is growing. I have a film career that is developing and two boys that keep me laughing. Throughout my journey I have moments when I take the time to appreciate how far I've come. I didn't get to this space mentally overnight, it took time, work and patience. But I've accepted that life will continuously have highs and lows but sometimes we get to experience some inordinate moments. It's those moments that make it all worthwhile. The great thing about being an entrepreneur, is it's a lifestyle that you get to create. It's about making sacrifices and tough choices and living your passion.

It's important for women to uplift, encourage and share information. I will say jumping into the entrepreneurship lane has not been easy but most fulfilling. If you take nothing from my story at least take this. First, let go of all your doubt! Don't let fear hold you hostage. Next, pursue your passion and follow your dreams. Just remember that dreams without goals are just dreams! So you want to have some goals and objectives. Finally, if it's something that you love doing, don't worry about how to make money because that will come.

Being an entrepreneur is not for everybody, because it often means long days, late nights, and a frugal lifestyle. It's tough starting out but for the few that keep going, the sky's the limit. As I watch my kids grow up I realize that time is precious so why not live the life you want. Be unapologetically you, live in your truth and trust the process.

LaRicia Nelson is walking her journey one chapter at a time. The talented social media marketer has reinvented herself again. With over 10 years of sales, marketing and event planning experience LaRicia decided to jump back into the entrepreneurship world with Twinn Media Group, LLC, a boutique agency that helps build brands through increasing online presence. She has also continued to pursue her passion for film and is building her credit as a producer. She has no plans on slowing down and to only go up from here. LaRicia is Designing+Her+Life.

Finding My Purpose

What is my purpose in life? What was I meant to do? What does God have in store for me and my life? Looking back on my life and everything I have been through, I can honestly say I have found my calling, which is becoming a published author. My journey on how I came to realize my purpose in life has been a struggle, but it was worth it. I have put my trust in God to direct me down the right path to my dream.

I started my journey when I was 16 years old. I just want to say for the record I love and admire my mom to the fullest. Raising two girls on her own, and with little help she deserves it all. There are just some things I will never understand that she went through; just as she would never understand the things I went through. I have been overweight for as long as I could remember, and being teased in school didn't help any, but hearing the backlash from my mom made it worse for me. Hearing my whole life that I won't amount to anything, made me lose sight of what my purpose in life is.

A few years ago, I was at a very low point in my life. I became severely depressed to the point where I questioned why I should live. During my moment of depression, I picked up a pen and a piece paper, and started writing. I started to feel somewhat better, but not my normal self. The day I realized I was meant to be here was when I was on my way to a job interview in Bethesda, MD. The red line train was running late, so there were a lot of people waiting. When the train finally arrived, and people started to pile on, the train got so full that something told me to just wait for the next train. As soon as the train pulled off, and got halfway into the tunnel it crashed with the train that was in front of it. In that very moment my depression went away, and I fought harder for what I wanted out of life, and to find my purpose.

After the incident with the train, I got my life back together. I found a job, started going to school, and even started writing a lot more than what I had did before. At this point I still had no idea what my purpose to become a writer was. All I could think about was that whatever God had in store for me I was sure I was ready. At that point in my life I was a very angry, young woman, and had no cares in world, so what happened next is what put me right back into depression. By this point I had lost my job because I was very angry and didn't care about anything. My family was starting to give up on me, and I had been constantly between homes. I finally decided at this point that I needed to get to the root of my anger and my depression. I sought out help and started to get my life back on track.

I am going to pause here because what I can say is, had I given up on myself I would not be here today. This last depression or so I thought, that took place for me was my absolute rock bottom. I actually tried to kill myself at this point. I thought I had no purpose. I hadn't accomplished anything, and I felt worthless. The night I tried to kill myself, I heard a voice, and that voice told me that it was not my time, and to pick myself up because something better was coming. So that's what I did, I picked myself up, found a new job, moved to a new state, and enjoyed life from there.

Let me tell you, it was not easy for me to get back up. I did the only thing I knew to do to ease my pain, which was to write and work.

The hardest part for me after my depression is self-blame. Self-blame is no fun, let me tell, but my tip for overcoming self-blame is to write down everything you blame yourself for not accomplishing and accomplish at least one of those goals at a time until you are not blaming yourself anymore. I promise this will make you feel complete. I am always so hard on myself, and never give myself the credit I deserve because I don't feel I deserve it. I am on a constant journey of finding myself, and becoming a better person. I started to notice a change in myself on my 25th birthday. I was driving to my grandmother's house and was at a red light, when I noticed a homeless man walking around with no shoes. I called him over to my car and told him to get in. As we were sitting in the car having a conversation, I realized in that moment that could have been me. I took the man to a hotel, gave him a pair of shoes that I had in the trunk of my car, bought him food, and told him to never give up on himself. I could have easily just kept driving past him and not have had a care in the world, but that day something said "Victoria help him". I gave this older gentleman my number and told him to find a way to contact me if he could, when he did, he explained to me that he had found a homeless shelter, found a job, and was saving his money so he could get his own place. He then thanked me for my kindness and my kind words.

After that day I have dedicated my time into helping others in need. If I have only a dollar, then I will give it to someone who does not have that dollar. At this point in my life I am fully aware of what my purpose in life is, but I am still trying to walk in a way God would approve. Where did I leave off? Right, so a year after my 25th birthday I had lost my job where I was working for over a year and half. When it first happened I was very positive, and told myself every day that I will find something better. Things were hard in the beginning but got a little easy as I still had money coming in. Granted I blew a lot of the initial money on my 26th birthday which was a bad choice on my part, but later made up for it. I felt my depression starting to kick back in, and again my family looked down on me. This time it was coming from my sister, and that hurt me the most. She stopped speaking to me for a while, would talk about me to her friends, and made me feel worse about myself than I already did.

So far it has been years at this point that I have been battling with depression, and this last time was my ultimate downfall with depression. I started cutting myself, drinking every day, and using sex as an escape for the pain. One night while I was cutting myself, I was listening to a gospel song by Kirk Franklin called "Let it Go", and though our situations are different, I can still relate to the song. I am lying there in the bed crying my eyes out and still trying to figure out why I haven't gotten anywhere with my writing or become a published author.? I have asked myself this question so many times and can't seem to figure it out. Could it be because I keep straying from the path that God has set for me? The more I listened to this song, the more I thought about my purpose.

After the crying and praying, I woke up the next morning with a new found purpose in life, and that was to pursue my dreams. I started to look for another job, and writing until my heart was healed. Writing has always been my escape from my reality, and it helped me through my most painful times.

After a few months of praying, applying, and going on countless interviews, God blessed me with a job. I worked as hard as I could, learned everything I needed to become successful, and I realized my heart was not content with just doing the same thing over and over again. The more I felt this way the more I started to not care about my job anymore. I know that's bad to say, but when God puts something in your heart, you have to go after it. That night I prayed for a better life, and God was leading me away from the job I was in.

Every night after work I went home and wrote at least one chapter a day just to fill my hole that was growing in my heart. Now this is where my life starts to take a turn. I am finally realizing my purpose in life is to follow my dreams through all of my hardships, pain, and struggle. At this point my writing urge started to grow so strong that I was at work writing instead of doing my work. God works in mysterious way. As I am writing in my book a nice gentleman walks in to get assistance. Now anybody in the store could have helped him, but there was a long wait and I decided to just help him. The nice gentleman and I were having a conversation, and I asked him what he did for a living. He said he was a writer and movie producer. I found that God had perfect timing because I was just telling my mother how I wanted to publish a book, and write a script, and here was this nice man who had already done that. So I am picking his brain on how I should go about putting my work out there, and he offered to read my work. In that moment God was pushing me towards my purpose, and let me tell you I was listening.

The only thing that was on my mind now was to follow my dreams of becoming an author. I'm still at this job full time, still unhappy, and trying to find something better all while writing. A few weeks after the nice man came into my store, a wonderful woman walked in, and was talking about a business she was opening. As the conversation went on she told me I would be perfect as the receptionist, and I said agreed and kept in contact. By this point I was praying hard, and grinding even harder for something new to come my way, and that day I met her I was given something new.

A few months go by, one chapter a day, and I have my second completed book. The only thing I needed to do was edit, add, remove, etc. I get an email one day from the woman who told me I would be a great receptionist to come in for orientation to her new business. This is where my test came, do I follow what God is telling me or do I continue to work a job that has left me unhappy? I struggled for days with my decision, until an incident at work happened, and I knew in that moment that it was time for me to get out. I decided to go to the orientation and I was happy I did. After the orientation I never went back to work, and that is when I started a new journey in my life. Follow your dreams, your heart, and what God is pushing you to do. Following him has pushed me to do things I never thought possible, and I am enjoying every moment of it. Writing is my passion, my dream, and my purpose. What's your passion? Your purpose? Your dream? God will see that you accomplish what you set out to do or be, just put your trust in Him, and pray every day.

    I started my new job on August 23, 2015, which was my birthday. I had become very happy in that moment. I was able to speak with the owner of the salon where I would be working and got to know her and what her accomplishments were. As we are talking I told her that my dream was to be a writer, and from there everything took off. God gave me my fuel and desire to be more than I am, and I have been following through with his plan. At every turn I was placed in the lives of people who were to get me to where I was going. After that conversation with her I knew in my heart that God placed me there for a reason. Since being there I have struggled a bit but I have been a lot happier with my struggle, because I knew that in the long run it would pay off. The completion of my first book is where I started. I did endless research on how to self-publish and how to publish with a traditional publisher. I decided that self-publishing would be my best option. I had to invest in myself in order to make my dream happen. I put every dollar I made into self-publishing my book. The more I chased my dream the more I started to struggle. By now I was not able to keep up with my rent or any other bills. I did not let that stop me or turn me away from my dream. I kept pushing. By doing so I became homeless with nowhere to go, and no one to turn to for help. Even still I kept writing and kept going after my dream. I prayed every day and every night that things would get better, and my prayer was answered. I found a publishing company to help with my self-publishing of my first book. I lost my place and had to relocate to a new state but I am not letting my struggles stop me from my dream. I kept pushing forward, I prayed, and I worked hard. My purpose in life is to face situations head on, and push through no matter what comes my way. I have learned to stay positive, to never give up on God, and to work hard no matter what. I am here today living my dream, following my dream, and following God's plans for me wherever they may take. I won't stop and I can't stop because stopping means I am giving up on myself, and that is one thing I refuse to do. Finding my purpose took a lot of heartache, loss of friends, and working through a lot of pain to get to the point in my life, where if something goes wrong I know that God is saying it was not meant for me. I challenge myself every day to try something new, to push myself to do something I have never done, and to continue the path of my purpose that God has set before me. I may not know where the road will lead, but with God I will follow blindly and be happy in the process. I will continue to think positive, and continue to walk in my truth. I was made for something bigger than me and when I stopped to listen to what God was trying to tell me, my life has been so much happier and stress free. Find your purpose, follow God, and trust that God will lead you to the right path.

Victoria Ross has been a writer since 9th grade. Currently working for Sprint Nextel Corporation in the Greenville, SC area, she has a website on WordPress where you can find her most current writings and new ideas.

Power of Choice

If you had told me as a child that in my twenties I would be a makeup artist living in America, I would have never believed you. I was born and raised in Malawi, a small country in the south east part of Africa where the weather is beautiful and the people are warm hearted. Going to college was exciting for someone like me who grew up in a somewhat strict African home. Like in most developing countries where education is not readily available, it is of the utmost importance for one to attain the highest level of education one can in order to be successful. Until recently the pursuit of creative careers was not really encouraged where I am from. Even though it was never verbalized, I knew that I was expected to achieve a high level of academic and professional excellence.

In my sophomore year of college my father was appointed as a foreign diplomat and my family moved to New York! For my siblings and I moving to America seemed like a dream come true. We could finally experience all the things we saw on television like Starbucks skinny lattes which was on top of my to-do list. I rejoined my family in New York after graduation to officially start my "adult life". Going to graduate school seemed like the obvious next step so a few months later I enrolled at the City College of New York to achieve a Master's degree in International Relations.

Up until this point in my life I had never really questioned my career path. I thought what I wanted was to achieve high academic success, work in a reputable field and have a career that would make my parents proud. However, what I experienced was completely different. About a month into my studies I started getting anxiety attacks everyday just before my classes. My heart would start racing, my head spinning and I would break into a sweat. The first couple of times this happened I told myself to suck it up. I figured I was just nervous and over reacting. Eventually I had to face the truth, I realized that I was physically manifesting my internal struggles. The truth was that I did not want to be there, I did not want to complete a two-year master's program. This was not what I wanted to do with my life. So after one semester I dropped out of Graduate school.

The depression soon followed. I felt stuck because I did not know how to continue with my life. 'How was I going to be successful? What career was I going to have?' And then there was the issue of telling my parents. I felt scared to admit that this path to my success that was in front of me was not what I truly wanted and that it caused me anxiety to stay on it.

I was also going through a spiritual evolution at the time. I had been a Christian my whole life. My parents took me to church as a child and when I got older I formed my own relationship with God based on my life experiences. Granted some years that relationship was stronger than others but there was always a connection there. There was something different about this time around though. My concept of God was beginning to expand, I was learning about ancient African spirituality and how it relates to my own faith. For the first time in my life I was experiencing spiritual cognitive dissonance. My concept of who and what God was was not matching up to the facts that I knew to be true about my African history.

I felt like what had previously been taught to me was not aligninwith this new enlightened person I was becoming. I found a new love for my culture and my people and could no longer identify with a religion that did not allow me to embrace that. I started doing my own research and I prayed that if what I was learning was false it would be to be revealed to me and that if it right I prayed for further clarification. Knowing that my faith went beyond my religious constraints helped me realize that there was more to me than just a great job and a career. I found courage knowing that I existed from a lineage of royalty and I owed it to myself and my people to go past the norm and really delve deep into what my calling was.

One day I was in the shower, where all great thinking happens and I started having the mother of a breakdown, ugly cry and all. I couldn't shake the feeling of being direction-less. I was working a part time job and getting by but I was really unhappy. So I prayed for direction. A couple days after the ugly cry bathroom scene I found a book by Debbie Macomber called "Knit Together." It stuck out to me because the tag line below the title was "discover Gods pattern for your life." This book was one of my answers to that prayer in the bathroom. The author uses her passion for knitting to describe how she found the courage to start writing and go on to become a bestselling author. She uses her story to guide and assist readers on how to find their purpose.

According to Debbie "God puts desires in our hearts through our dreams, through our passions, and through what brings us joy." She then challenges the reader to take a look at the passion in our purpose and ask "what is it that gets me excited?' "What do I love to do?"

This was the easy part because I knew what I was passionate about. I have been in love with makeup and beauty. My mother bought me my first black eye liner and an eye shadow palette as a preteen and I was hooked. In college I did makeup on my friends for all their big dates, parties and the huge college senior's dinner. I didn't realize it then but this was me being a makeup artist and living out my passion. Once I had discovered that this was what I was passionate about, the pieces started to fall into place. I went online and bought my first brush set and some products and began practicing my skills that I was learning online through YouTube video tutorials.

"When you want something, all the universe conspires to help you achieve it" – the Alchemist. I am a living testament of the truth in this quote. Shortly after my decision I got a call from Aliki, one of my graduate school friends. She was calling to check up on me and I informed her about this great new decision to follow my dreams to become a makeup artist. Turns out she had been working with a small business Cosmetics Company based in Harlem called OmoSade skincare, that was selling cosmetics and African skincare for women of color and they were looking for a makeup artist. When God answers your prayers through people, I call them vessels. To me they are an embodiment of God working on your behalf through them. I am grateful for the vessels in my life. You will know when you have met one when they assist you in achieving Gods purpose for your life.

Now that I was officially working as a makeup artist and selling cosmetics I got a little brave. I finally told my parents what I wanted to do. As expected my parents were disappointed. My dad felt like I was making a mistake, in his opinion the beauty industry was a career for people who failed to make it through the corridors of higher learning and it was not what he had envisioned for his daughter. Mum I felt was mainly confused about how I intended to support myself through this dream. I accepted their opinions but I knew I had to make my own decisions.

As my skills as an artist developed, my purpose became clearer in terms of the service I was meant to do. I realized that the main reason that I was given a dream is so I can help others live theirs. I fell in love with doing makeup because of what it did for me. On days were I felt insecure a little mascara and lip-gloss did a lot to boost my confidence and uplift my spirits. I realized I wanted to serve God by making other people feel good about themselves. I wanted the women I worked on to be empowered and enjoy their own beauty in their lives. Most importantly, my purpose was to touch women of color especially in Africa and improve their self-perception and ultimately assist them in realizing their potential. From this came the idea to create a beauty brand and start a self-love movement, through which I can fulfill my purpose.

Once I understood the what, it was time to figure out the how. My job fell through a few months after my family returned to Malawi. It is hard adjusting to independence as a young adult but even harder trying to do so in one of the toughest cities in the world with no fixed income and a dream. Once again I had to make a choice, this time it was whether to stay and continue to pursue my dreams in New York or leave and follow my family. I was not sure which way to go. On one hand I felt that I could be a successful makeup artist at home and be able to live out my purpose there but also felt that I was not ready. There was still a lot that I had not done to be able to successfully execute my dream of establishing my own cosmetics line.

My next vessel came in the form of a tall handsome New Yorker named Ramel. I was just about ready to give up when we met. We exchanged life stories and I learned he was pursuing his dream as an artist too. I told him where I was in my journey that I was about leave and return to Malawi. In response he asked me if I was comfortable going back knowing I had given it my best shot. The answer was no. I knew I was giving up because I was scared. I feared if I stayed and tried to make my dreams come true in America the road was going to be too hard. However, I knew I had to believe in myself and make the necessary sacrifices to get to where I wanted to be. I was not sure how I was going to make it but I knew I wanted to achieve my dreams more than I wanted to be comfortable.

So I stayed! The years that followed were not easy. On the purpose journey there is no comfort zone to fall into. You are constantly taking risks and allowing yourself to go through it because you know that what you are working towards is bigger that you. I understood that if I was to experience true joy in my life I had to give accomplishing my dreams a shot and stick to it. I went into business for myself as a freelance makeup artist, building clientele and getting paid for the work that I did. It was hard as the jobs were not frequent but it felt great to know that I was actually doing it. My landlord was getting frustrated with the late payments so I got kicked out of my first apartment. This was hard to go through especially when you are constantly being reminded by family that you could just leave, abandon ship and just come home. I know my family wanted the best for me but I could not help but feel angry. Every time we spoke and they insisted that I leave and go home I would get disappointed because I did not feel that I was being supported. The tougher things got, the more I persevered. I could not afford anything in a descent location so I found a barely finished one bedroom apartment in the Bronx. I moved in that winter and after the first day the heat got cut off. My landlord assured me he would have it fixed but he never did. I was in that cold apartment for a month. I didn't buy a bed because I knew I was going to leave that environment as soon as I could. Those cold nights on the floor of that apartment taught me so many lessons that may help you on your journey.

It taught me that I was willing to give up comfort in order stay the course and follow through for what I believed in. You have to be able to make sacrifices and prioritize what is really important. Having the cutest clothes or latest gadgets was not important to me. As long as I could still go to work, see my clients and have a roof over my head, I was happy. It taught me that I made the right choice. Albeit a difficult one, I was happy in my decision. I cried some nights but it was only for the moment. Only to allow myself to feel the pain and use it to push me into the direction of my dreams.

It taught me to trust the process. I learned to trust that the purpose God had put in my heart was not in vain but for a reason. This is where I feel it is important to attach your dreams to service. Money cannot be the source of the inspiration for the dreams you have because you can easily give up when the money is low. Knowing that there are people waiting on you to achieve my dream, and that your temporary sacrifice will bring joy to someone else's life will help you get through the tough nights.

The more I stuck it out over the years the more detailed my plan got. I was getting clearer on how I was going to live out my purpose. During the past couple of years the Cosmetics industry, propelled by social media platforms such as Instagram, You tube and Twitter has seen tremendous growth. I was inspired by what I saw on these platforms and I knew I had a place in the blogger sphere and in the cosmetics business. I loved that social media had provided me with the ability to reach the women that I wanted to reach without physically being there. I too wanted to launch my blog but I came up with a million reasons why I could not. "You have an accent'. 'You don't have the right equipment', And then there is the classic "What would people think?"

Underlining it all was my own insecurity that I never managed to live past. Even though I was on a mission to help women find the beauty in themselves I was struggling to see my own beauty. The message of self-love is easy to preach but it is even harder to follow. Total self-confidence and self-love is a thing that requires more than just being told that you are beautiful. It encompasses total self-acceptance. Acknowledging and accepting your weaknesses and loving yourself regardless. I realized I was actually insecure about what I looked like. I had struggled with my weight in college and even though I had worked hard to shed the pounds, I still had to work on shedding the emotional baggage and insecurity. I started to actively work on loving myself, including forgiving myself for things I felt guilty for, accepting my perceived flaws and changing the narrative. I began to see myself as the titles I aspired to be; blogger, makeup artist, brand owner and get rid of all the limiting beliefs that told me I could not be what I wanted to be.

Armed with my growing self-confidence I was ready to create my footprint in the beauty industry. I had struggled for a long time about what I was going to call my brand because I did not want to come off shallow or vain. It was important that I still communicated the essence of my purpose in my brand name. Zani is the last part of my name Thokozani and it is what my American friends and family call me so Zani Beauty felt so natural to me. I decided to google it to see if it had been taken by anyone. The meaning of the name Zani came up and I was shocked to find the relevance and connection that I personally had to it. According to the urban dictionary, Zani "is the true African lotus blossom and gift from God." It goes on to describe Zani as someone who has to endure a lot but the story that is their life will inspire others. I loved it! I received this definition as my final confirmation that I had made the right choice. Everything came full circle after reading this definition and I understood that there are no mistakes in life. That everything I have gone through is all relevant to the completion of God's plan.

The choice I made to follow my own path and

live a purpose driven life is one that has seen me through a lot of highs and lows. The journey is still continuing and I have only scratched the surface but I feel so blessed to have been given this mission in my life. I welcome all the lessons that are to come. I am returning to Malawi after six years of being away. This is crucial for me spiritually because my connection to my culture, my ancestors and to God is deeper than it has ever been. I am excited as a business woman to introduce my brand to my people. I am looking forward to using the lessons that I have learned here to begin the execution of my purpose.

So I encourage you, to go boldly in the direction of your dreams. Make the choice to find and fulfil the purpose of your existence and make it time and time again.

Thokozani Phiri, is a 27year old Malawian skincare and beauty expert . She has worked with brands such as Lancome and L'occitane . She credits her walk with God as being the reason behind her passion for beauty and female empowerment. In her spare time she writes about spirituality and achieving inner and outer beauty on her website www.thezaniedit.com.

Passion Leads to Purpose

"We all are a sum total of our life experiences"
-Sandra A. Cooley

    I am a non-traditionalist who became a CEO, Author and Philanthropist. I am a product of a divorced household. This led me to live in multiple households throughout my childhood. After my parents' divorce, I lived with my mother until I was eight, then with my father and his parents until I was twelve, then with my father and his third wife until I was fourteen and then finally with my mother's mother, Vivian. This may seem to be a bit unstable but it was the most stable environment in the world to me teaching me the most valuable lessons throughout life. Since my mother was a singer, there was entertainment daily in our household and by entertainment I mean music, harmony, "real" musicians, lots of rehearsals and performances. This was my life, every day. I woke up and went to sleep hearing music. I lived for the music. As a kid, I couldn't wait to go to rehearsal with my mother to hear the harmony of the Flirtations (my mom's group). I wanted to be a part of the Flirtations (and who didn't?). They were that good. I would close my eyes and pretend my mother was calling my name as she received her Grammy. As I got older, I would write songs and sing but I wasn't good enough to make it out of a career. However, I was confident in knowing that I knew talent. I knew which artist(s) had the potential to make it. I could hear it from the very first note or from the first four bars of a rap line. On the other hand, I knew there was something that was tugging at my soul; it was intangible but I didn't know what to call it or what to do with that feeling.

    As time went by, I'm now in college doing "the right thing" while suffering from inner turmoil of unhappiness. I found myself sitting in college knowing I didn't belong there. Yet, I followed the "wolf pack theme", "Go to college, and get a good job with an IRA 401K so you can plan for retirement. Although I was doing just that very same thing at the time, I wasn't being fulfilled. I felt so empty. I felt as if I was on auto pilot being controlled by someone else's destiny. It seemed as if every professor was the teacher from the Visine commercial, mono toned and dry. My unhappiness was like craving for a certain food, but instead I decided to settle for something else just because I was hungry. And when you don't get what you craved for its like having a bottomless stomach, nothing will satisfy you until you get what you desire. And there I was being unhappy in my young life. A friend of mine told me once that "sometimes doing the right thing isn't always the right thing to do." So, I did two more semesters, one studying abroad (which I loved) and the other miserably failing my classes; eventually, my nonfulfillment led to academic probation and failing out of school.

After failing out of school, I started searching for jobs but couldn't find anything. So one day my cousin said his job had an opening (at a camera store) as a sales person and would I be interested in working there. I said yes and started the following week. I liked the job because of my colleagues but in my heart I knew it wasn't for me. I needed the income at the time so I did what I had to do; not knowing that something greater would come from "the camera store." At the time I had no actual plans for my life, I was just going with the flow but, God had something greater for me. He was just waiting on me to start. As my great aunt Sandra says, "if you do what you need to do in the natural, the supernatural will take place." The natural is simply applying the principles: See, Speak and Do.

After the camera store, I moved out of town to accept a job as a salesperson at a bank. I was excited at the time to make more money than I ever had, but soon I lacked enthusiasm due to a bottomless stomach. Again, I followed the "wolf pack theme" and settled for something else just because I was hungry. I was so stressed. I was forcing myself to make sales on something I cared absolutely nothing about, and it showed. I remembered it like it was yesterday. There it was, my name plastered on the big white board listed "second to last" in the whole department...I'll never forget it. I was ashamed and embarrassed. I said to myself I have to do better and better meant in my overall life. My everyday life was being affected by what was in the inside, nonfulfillment. I was stressed and unhappy at the job and it showed through my work. As Simon Sinek plainly puts it, "Working hard for something we don't care about is called stress; working hard for something we love is called passion." Finally, that moment of clarity happened. One day, I was lying in my bed looking at the ceiling saying to myself "this is not what I am supposed to be doing with my life" At that very moment, I realized I had to find something I loved to do and with a purposeful meaning.

    I began to reflect on who I was as a person. I have always been a person of what and why, especially as a kid, but mainly because I didn't like adults telling me what to do without a real reason. Therefore, I would constantly ask, why do I have to do this? What's the purpose? Can I do this? What's the reason? Or why should I? However, I did ask myself "what am I passionate about?" Although they are both different, you do need them both to pursue your dreams. I believe at some point in everyone's life we have questioned ourselves one way or the other asking "what am I put on this earth to do?" And "how do I discover it?" It simply means focusing on one thing and letting everything else fall into place.

    Here's how: Ask yourself "What am I passionate about?"
Passion is a word that is not often used in

everyday life. If you actually took a survey, you may find that not everyone really knows what passion is. It's often used in pastime. It's more of a cliché rather than the primary focus. Some people may say that passion is a hobby or a leisure activity and may not see it as a reality. So, what is passion? Passion is "something that you love to do." It is the "what?" It's what gets you so excited that you can talk about it for hours, and it feels like it's only been fifteen minutes. In the movie Sister Act, Whoopi Goldberg tells Lauryn Hill, "If you wake up and think about singing, if you go to sleep and think about singing then that's what you're supposed to be doing."

    The day I was looking at the ceiling thinking to myself "this is not what I am supposed to be doing with my life" I simply asked myself several questions "what am I passionate about?" "What do I wake up and fall asleep thinking about? And "If I got paid $2.50 an hour to do it, what would I do?" At that moment, I realized that I had been wasting my time and energy just for a paycheck that made me miserable and unhappy. Often times in life we settle for a paycheck and don't do what we love to do. We allow "life's transactions" to dictate our destiny and don't follow the compass of our passion. Imagine this instead: You get up early for a job you dislike or even hate. You fight traffic for hours to and from work. Your boss and co-workers annoy you; you leave work every day for lunch hoping to get a peace of mind for an hour... just to get a check. However, if you got paid $2.50 an hour to do that one thing you love…oh what a joy it would be. You would wake up happy every morning being that football coach you've always desired to be. You would be happy to be a florist. You would be happy to be a writer. You would be happy to be a kindergarten teacher. You would be happy to inspire others with your poems and songs… gladly doing it all for $2.50 an hour. Wouldn't it be nice?

Think of it this way: Passion is the engine of the car. It's what gets you started. It's the feeling and emotion that burns within you. Once you find your passion it will then lead you to your purpose in life.

Start Brainstorming

The day I discovered my passion for $2.50 an hour, my eyes opened not literally but figuratively and I said "the music industry." I thought to myself, I was birthed from a songstress and I loved everything about music so I couldn't go wrong. From there, I started to write down everything I thought I could do to get in the business. On my list, (which was minimal) I wrote singing and song writing but thought 'nah' because I was just okay at it. I didn't play an instrument. I could carry a note or two but not too far. I knew I wouldn't want to sign myself if I was on the other side of the table.

As I started to brainstorm, I started reflecting on my mother's singing career: Why she never made it? She was almost there but never reached the stardom status. She sung and performed with the best in business at that time, but what was missing? The group was "hella-fied" singers, they looked the part, they had the sound but something wasn't adding up. And there it was, I found the needle in the hay stack, "Management." I said I will manage artists. I realized that my mother's group didn't have the right management to bring them to the next level.

Overwhelmed with my passionate discovery, I started to write down all the missing pieces I saw from my mother's group and thought about how I would apply it to my own artist, if I had one. All I had on my vision list was the music industry, management and a few ideas. Now I'm thinking, what do I do from here? I did not realize the power I was putting into the universe by writing it down. According to Habakkuk 2:2, "write the vision, make it plain unto tables that he may run that readeth it."

As a few months went by and now I'm visiting my hometown and I ran into a childhood friend. We began to catch up and he stated that he would be in the city where I lived visiting his brother. I accepted the invitation to his brother's house and his brother and I started to talk about the music industry and realized that we had a common interest in managing artists and later decided to start a management company.

This was the outcome of brainstorming by myself and with others. It's important to share what you do and/or what you're looking to do because you never know who is who or who knows who. On the other hand, you must be careful who you tell your vision to. Many ideas have been stolen and have not come into fruition because of who they have told or what the other person may have said to put fear in them.

Take Action and Keep Moving

Now that I'd found my passion, the wheels began to turn and the plan was now in motion. We had gone on to produce numerous concerts, events and found the artist who would take the world by storm. He was a talented artist and a good kid. He didn't smoke or drink. He was the artist that record labels dream of, trouble-less. He was always on time for rehearsal. He was a hard worker with a strong desire to make it.

Then one night I got a phone call from my business partner's wife stating that my artist was killed and his girlfriend had been shot in the head and he was shot in his face several times by his first cousin. I held the phone, but I didn't hear anything. I had no heart beat and my body was numb. It took everything out of me. I felt as if I was hit by a Mack Truck. Thank God his girlfriend survived to tell who the shooter was. She said as his cousin was shooting him he kept saying "Oh so you're a star now, nigga." For the life of me, I couldn't understand how this could happen to the best kid in the world. It turned my dream into a nightmare. I felt that life had let me down and all of this because of jealously. I felt like I had failed life's greatest test. How could something that gave me so much joy bring me excruciating pain? I didn't want to deal with music again. I threw in the towel and moved back home.

As time healed my wounds, I knew that I had to overcome this adversity. I had to get up and try again. I couldn't allow my situation to destroy the promise God had for me. I believe that there is value in tragedy, failure and hardship. It's all about life's lessons and how we will deal with it. As my grandmother Vivian says, "You learn two ways in life: knowledge or experience" That's why you should never be afraid of hardships. It's about getting up and starting over. No one has a perfect life. My tragedy made me stronger. This was a building block for the roads to come. I had to accept that hardship is a part of life and I had to try again if I wanted to win.

Whatever you put your mind to, do it and don't stop. Don't allow hardships to affect your destiny, just keep going no matter what. It's all worth it in the end. The biggest obstacle that keeps most of us from succeeding is stopping when we come to a bump in the road. This paralyzes our progress, and causes us to be stuck in the same position for years. Therefore, I had decided not to be that person. I had to welcome and embrace the process of life with the good and the bad to get to my purpose.

Purpose: It's not for you

Getting to my purpose was a little bit challenging for me because I knew what I was passionate about, but I didn't know my purpose. I was living the life: I had a great career and living the dream of a young single woman doing everything that I had desired at that time. However, I was so engulfed by my surroundings that I was blinded by the hype. I was hanging out with celebrities, going on tours, traveling around the world and staying in five star hotels and yes that was exciting to me at the time but eventually it started going downhill. I was so focused on the organization's vision; I lost mine in the meantime.

My initial vision was to find my purpose once I found my passion. It took me a couple of years to realize that time had passed me by. I had to take a few steps back to realize that life was trying to get my attention. So, I started reflecting on my past experiences. What was I good at? What do people need me for? What am I supposed to be doing? And what do people think I'm great at? I realized that people always call on me to help them connect with others. Then a light switch went off…if people are always calling me for this specific thing then this is what I'm supposed to be doing. And that is helping others to achieve their goals. This is how I became "the connector." I wasn't afraid to ask.

In the end, your purpose in life is to bless others. Give and it shall be given unto you. I hope and pray as you were reading my story that it has shifted your mind and desire to find your passion, to brainstorm, keep going and never stop moving to find your purpose. As TD Jakes says "Your passion is what connects you to your purpose". Keep striving as I'm still doing and "May your journey on earth be fulfilled with divine purpose."

A non-traditionalist turned CEO, philanthropist, and author, Kelly McHenry has shaped her life experiences into a powerful guide. As Executive Chair and Co-Founder of PINK House, a personal development academy for young ladies, McHenry has taken the skills and experiences she has learned along the way to grow and enhance her reach to the youth of her beloved city. As a New Orleans native, McHenry's determination, bold nature and powerful voice has lead her in to a community of influence expanding her power as a leader to those around her.

Setbacks Are Setups (For Greatness)

We all go into our careers after college with excited energy and this American dream in our heads that now that we have graduated from college and landed a position using our degree that everything will flow from there and we'll go on to rise in the company and build this great resume and make lots of money, have kids, get married and have the white picket fence that we have always been told about. Well my story about my career hasn't quite gone that way. What I want you to take away from my story is that number one when you let go and let God take control of your life and stop thinking it's all on you, amazing things will manifest that you never dreamed of. I also want you to take a few life lessons on being prepared for anything that can possibly happen, having some stress relieving techniques that you actively use in your life when the going gets tough and never forget about yourself and your personal dreams, goals, and business ideas while working for other people's companies. Lastly I want you to be inspired by the intentions I set for myself and how they became reality so that you understand the power of setting focused, clear intentions for what you want for your life.

Many people tell me that they never really knew what they wanted to do with their life once they finished college and I've never been able to relate. I knew at the ripe young age of 10 that I was going to be a fashion designer when I grew up therefore I've been setting clear intentions for my life since adolescence. I was a very artistic child, who loved drawing and painting. I also loved shopping and keeping up with the latest fashion trends more than anything. I'll never forget the first time my mother dropped me off to hang out with my friends in the mall without her. I was in the 3rd grade and she gave me $40 to spend and I will never forget the trendy polka dot 80's Madonna inspired look I bought from the Children's place! I don't remember a time in my life that I didn't have a passion for fashion. Therefore, it made perfect sense to pursue fashion design as a career. I went to college in Atlanta, Georgia at Clark Atlanta University my first year. I transferred to another school the second, still in Atlanta, called Bauder College. This turned out to be a good decision because Bauder was much more of the hands on fashion education that I was looking for.

After finishing my Associates degree at Bauder, I quickly moved to NYC to find a job within the fashion industry. At that time there were plenty of positions in the industry and it was very easy to land a job. Times have changed drastically since! My first position was a pattern guide editor and pattern checker for McCall's pattern company in NYC. I was living in the guest room at my college roommate's mother's house deep in Jamaica, Queens close to JFK airport and commuting on the subway in and out of Manhattan daily. I hated this because it was a long commute and I was used to being in my car in Atlanta.

About 2 months after starting this position I left and accepted a position as a Technical Designer with a children's licensing company with offices in NYC as well as offices located in a big warehouse in Bayonne, NJ. I was now commuting by driving from Queens all the way to NJ every single day. It was horrible. I spent sooooo much time in my car! I ended up getting an apartment by myself in NJ right outside of Manhattan and was so proud of myself for being able to hold down a place by myself straight out of college in the NYC metroplex.

Eventually my job would require me to work a few days in the NYC office and a few days in New

Jersey office. Once I started spending more time in NYC I really wanted a position in the city and I wanted to get out of the Technical Design role and into a true design position. At that point I took a position with another children's company where I stayed for close to 3 years and it was a very nice place to work as I landed an Associate Designer position. I had set my intentions on landing a design position. I reached a point where I was ready to move up to the next level but realized that people stayed at the company for so long and they didn't have a high turnover rate. Therefore, it made me feel that in order to grow I would have to stay at the company forever and be stuck doing the same thing until one of the people in the positions I was interested in left the company. I had an overwhelming feeling that I was supposed to be doing something bigger and greater with my time so I began to look for another position. This won't be the last time I have this overwhelming feeling that I'm bigger than whatever situation I'm in. Every time in my life that I've had this feeling and put intentions into the universe that I wanted to move on to something bigger and better, it's always happened for me and I'm so thankful for this fact.

The next position I accepted and I thought that "I'm bigger than this" place ended up not working out well so I quickly hit the pavement to seek another position. The lesson I learned in this situation is that the grass is not always greener on the other side. Every company you go to and position you accept will have its ups and downs. There's no perfect position or perfect company.

My next position was probably one of my favorite positions in my career. I was hired by a startup company, who had the license to design, manufacture, and sell to retailers an all new DKNY kids clothing line, where I was responsible for designing the girl's 7-16 portion of the collection. By this time, I was about 25 years old and this was probably the height of my career. I learned so much, had so much creative freedom, met amazing people that are now lifelong friends that feel like family and worked really hard in the process. Most of the experience was working late, late nights, weekends, all the time. I worked a lot on this job. But it didn't feel horrible because I loved the product that I was designing and the people that I worked with who also worked long hours right along by my side. Unfortunately, after 2 years the parent company from France decided to close the doors because the business wasn't performing up to the standards of the extremely aggressive initial business plan to have an extreme amount of high end children's apparel license deals within a very short period of time.

Remember I said I worked hard at this company and a lot of hours, late nights, weekends, etc. The day we all lost our jobs I learned that no matter how hard you work and hours you put in, you can lose your job in the blink of an eye. Therefore, it's super important to live within your means, save money so that you have a cushion in case something happens and never let yourself get to comfortable.

This was my first experience being let go or laid off from any job and it was pretty scary especially living in the extremely expensive NYC metro area. I filed for unemployment for the first time…but little did I know it wouldn't be my last time filing in my lifetime. I always feared being laid off because I feared being able to survive on the amount of money unemployment gave you especially when dealing with the New York City prices of everything. That summer I learned that it really wasn't that hard to adjust financially after being laid off if you aren't living beyond your means. I quickly looked over my monthly spending and decided where I needed to cut back in order to survive on unemployment and it wasn't hard to decide what I needed to cut back on. I cut back on eating out, buying clothes and hanging out partying where I'd most likely buy alcohol. I only ended up being on unemployment for a few months but in the end I felt much more confident and less fearful when it came to the topic of being laid off. This experience showed me that I had it all along and God will never let me go without so there never was a reason to fear in the first place. It honestly was a very liberating feeling not to have to be at a job at a certain time every day for those few months I didn't work. I really loved that feeling and wondered how could I make every day feel like this in my future but still be able to provide for myself. I ended up quickly working on my portfolio over the summer and traveled a little to see my family. I got laid off probably in the beginning of July and accepted a new position as a Sr. Designer for another children's company by the end of August. I didn't even stay at this company a year because it wasn't a good fit. The product was extremely boring to design which was a complete 360 from the interesting product I was now used to designing at DKNY. After about 8 or 9 months, I left to start a position as a design director for a Juniors bottoms company.

This was my first time actually being able to hire my own staff and manage a team which was a great experience that I had no idea that I was ready for. The way I got the job was by a head hunter reaching out to me about the position and my first reaction was, "I'm not ready to be in a director role yet." But she believed differently and said, "yes you are." This was one moment in my life that I can remember someone seeing something in me that I didn't even see in myself. She saw a natural born leader that was meant to lead people and I had no idea that this is what I was supposed to be doing with my life. This taught me that my plans and Gods plans don't always line up and that sometimes we tend to think too small and ask for things too small when God has huge plans for us and when we pray we need to pray big. Meaning ask for exactly what you want no matter how big or outlandish it may seem. Set clear focused intentions. It also taught me that God won't give you more than you're ready for. Even when you don't think you're ready, he knows he's prepared you for the task or he wouldn't give it to you. Don't fear a blessing that seems too large. Boldly say thank you to God for blessing you with the opportunity, grab the bull by the horns and get the job done that God ordained for you to do, and do your best at it.

This position ended up being amazing for my career because it was the first position that allowed me to travel for extensive amounts of time overseas to factories. I traveled for 2 weeks at a time every few months to China by myself to work with the factories to make sure our samples got completed before market where the sales team needed to be able to show them to buyers of retail stores in order for the line to get into stores. Unfortunately, this position only lasted about a year before I got laid off because the company cut back financially due to the climate of business and the economy at the time. This was around the 2008 housing industry collapse when many people were losing their jobs in the USA. I had just bought a condominium a year prior but I wasn't really freaked out about the fact that I now had a mortgage and no job since this wasn't my first layoff. Due to my first layoff experience my faith was stronger and I didn't fear a financial set back.

This layoff happened during the Spring, therefore the timing wasn't bad because the weather was nice. In my head I thought I'd pick up some freelance work and travel in between contracts. What I didn't realize was that I went through a pretty horrible personal situation that I really hadn't dealt with and taken the time to heal from. What made me realize that this time was what I really needed was when the veterinarian told me that I had to put my cat to sleep. They diagnosed the cat with diabetes and said she needed a blood transfusion because her kidneys were failing. Putting her down broke my heart and spun me into a very low emotional place that sparked me to realize my feelings about another loss I suffered around the same time. As a result, I took this time to deal with my grief for both of those situations and told myself I need to take it easy on myself and let go of feeling like I had to chase a new job since I wasn't working. I picked up freelance work, and collected unemployment and everything ended up working out just fine. My faith was strong in trusting that everything was going to be ok with this time now being my second experience being laid off and having to live off of unemployment.

This situation taught me that we as humans often coast through life moving from the next thing to the next just trying to keep up and most times don't stop to heal properly when we go through things. Sometimes people have to stop to realize that their life and the things they go through and losses they experience have a much larger impact on them mentally and emotionally than they realize. In order to move forward in a healthy way healing is so important and necessary. That job will always be there and if not another one will be but your mental, spiritual and physical wellbeing must be put first or you won't end up performing well at that job. The mind, body and spirit are all connected and it's very important to take loving care of each part of you to be a productive person and if that means taking time off when you're going through something then take the time off. You only get one you, take care of you.

By the beginning of the summer I had accepted a position at another company that bought the DKNY license after the last company went under. This company was a company that I had heard many crazy stories about over the years and never had a desire to work for due to this. But since

I wasn't working and they agreed to the hefty annual salary that I requested I took a chance and started working there. I was responsible for designing the girls 7-16 collection again but this time I had a whole team that I managed to help me. This was not an easy company to work for or position to be in, it was a very stressful place to work. There was a lot of negative energy there, people speaking to people in disrespectful ways, shouting matches were common, amongst many other things that wasn't appropriate for a professional environment. During this time, I started experiencing very sharp but weird stomach pains and having all kinds of weird issues and feelings happening in my stomach. I eventually went to a specialist who diagnosed me with Ulcerative Colitis, an inflammatory bowel disease.

Though they say they aren't sure what causes this incurable disease, they do know that stress plays a major part in triggering flare ups of the disease. As a result, I had to drastically change my diet and health habits. It was during this time that I stopped eating dairy products. One of my co-workers on me team at the time was also a yoga teacher and she told me I really needed to start doing yoga because I needed to do something to help keep my stress level low. As a result, I started taking yoga classes and it quickly became my exercise of choice whenever I worked out. The company ended up laying off my entire team later that year to bring another entire team in as a result of the new Vice President they hired. Take notice to the irony of this story and it's timing and how I literally got sick from the stress of this position just to end up without a job within a year of getting sick. The lesson learned here is you have to stay on top of your health, wellbeing and stress level before it gets too late. Don't wait until something major goes wrong with your body due to stress, work on stress management activities just because to avoid it affecting your health. Remember, mind, body and spirit come first and foremost no matter what. God didn't put us here to worry and stress out. We have to do our best to get things done and work hard but we have to know that we can't let things get to us and tear us up inside because that's only hurting us internally. We have to give everything to God, even foreseen issues to stress over at work and trust that he will work out whatever we are worried about because he has a plan for all things including our work responsibilities.

    This layoff happened around maybe the beginning of November right before the holidays. Therefore, I took full advantage of the timing and spent a lot of time in upstate New York with family and also traveled to North Carolina to visit family and had a great Thanksgiving and Christmas that year. Now that I had been laid off numerous times it wasn't such a big deal anymore. I learned quickly what to do financially during these times by basically only paying for the basics and cutting back on many things and made sacrifices by not doing certain things I was used to doing often such as getting my nails done, shopping and eating out all of the time. I was excited to have a break from working and wanted to take full advantage of the time. I had started reading a lot of books about branding yourself and was trying to figure out what it truly was that I wanted to do on my own in regards to starting a business. God started putting people in my life that helped drive this entrepreneurial spirit and I truly felt in my heart that I wasn't put here to work for someone else for the rest of my life and needed to figure out what it was that I was supposed to start a business doing on my own. I slightly feared working for myself while living in such an expensive place but through the people I was meeting at the time I saw people doing exactly what I dreamed of doing by working for themselves and maintaining a decent lifestyle in the NYC metroplex. I wasn't eager to find a new job. But instead as soon as the New Year rolled around I started getting many phone calls from recruiters telling me about job openings which was a blessing. One of the companies a headhunter called me about was a major department store located in Texas. I expressed I wasn't interested because I was not going to move to Texas and had no interest whatsoever to move to Texas. They convinced me to allow them to at least send my resume and I agreed.

The recruiter quickly called me to say that one of the directors out of the 2 divisions she sent my resume to wants to meet me in NYC for an interview while he was in NYC on business for the week. This was a snowstorm day and I remember wrapping up really good and heading to the city for the interview where I was met by a short, quirky Italian man in the lobby of his hotel where he interviewed me. The interview went well. He said he wanted to arrange for me to fly to Texas for more interviews with other people and wanted me to do a project to present on the trip. Despite my previous angst and lack of desire to move to Texas or even consider moving to Texas, once I met this man I had a feeling that if a personality like his could maintain in Texas it may not be that bad. He didn't give me what I expected I'd see when I saw people from Texas. He was more of the type of personality I'd expect to see in NYC so that was comforting.

I ended up going to Texas, getting stuck there due to ice storms, received a job offer and found an apartment all in one week. One month later the company paid to have movers pack my stuff and move it to my new apartment in Dallas. They also transported my car. This company ended up being a very different situation than I was used to because this was my first time working with buyers number one, and secondly my first time working at a place where the company bought product from clothing companies in the marketplace in addition to what the designers designed. It made it feel like it was a design competition, which I didn't like. Otherwise, it was a nice place to work.

Less than a year after I started with the company they brought in a new CEO. He began to make his mark on the company by making many changes. Usually when these situations happen layoffs typically will follow which is exactly what happened. They had several rounds of lay-offs and I got laid off during the second round. It happened during the summer, so I decided I wasn't eager to find another job and would take the time to enjoy the summer. The craziest thing is the one thing that I was most afraid of when I accepted this position was the thought of potentially getting laid off in a city with very minimal fashion industry positions. Getting laid off in NYC isn't that big of a deal because there always are so many apparel company options but this was new for me. I learned that God won't give you more than you can handle but he will give you what you fear the most to push you to increase your faith in him and live a fearless life. God didn't put us here to worry, that is His job as I said earlier in the story.

During the time that I wasn't working I decided to go to a yoga teacher training to get certified to teach. This was a life changing experience that allowed me to soul search and completely changed my life. Once I finished training I started teaching at the studio I trained with. I eventually had many people asking me if I could teach them private yoga lessons. I agreed and started teaching where ever I could. I taught in people's offices, my loft downtown, outside at parks, wherever I could teach, I taught and loved it. This was the first time in my life that people were paying me directly for a service and it felt great! I had developed the entrepreneur bug and felt like maybe this was the answer I was searching for when I was trying to figure out what type of business I wanted to start during my last layoff. Once the summer rolled around and people started traveling my business completely slowed down. As a result, I decided to travel for this entire summer as I knew opportunities to do such things don't happen often in life and I wanted to take full advantage of this free time.

The first place I went during that summer of extensive travel was Jamaica with my girlfriends on a girls trip. One of my friends brought a friend of hers on the trip from Hawaii and after hearing that I was a yoga teacher the woman asked me if I had ever heard of BUTI yoga and I hadn't. She pulled up a video on YouTube to show me and I lost my mind and immediately was obsessed with BUTI Yoga as soon as I saw it. There were women doing yoga to upbeat modern music while incorporating African dance moves within the yoga poses. I immediately decided I had to learn how to teach this form of yoga. I had clients who were requesting that I teach them yoga to rap music and I couldn't figure out how to, it didn't seem like the two went together, until I discovered BUTI Yoga! I immediately went to the BUTI Yoga website to find out when there would be a teacher training that I could take.

I decided I would attend training the first weekend in August in Denver, CO. Training ended up being very intense and definitely not easy, but worth it. I was sore for several days after the training. Being that my brother and his family live in Denver I stayed and hung out with them for a few days. During this time, I received a text from someone in Dallas, that I had told previous to my summer travel that I was looking for studio space to rent for my own yoga classes. She said she had a friend who was a Zumba teacher looking for space to teach as well. I connected with her friend once I arrived back to Dallas and she had already found studio space in a shared space. I joined and decided to prepare to truly launch my yoga business. I paid an artist to design a logo for the business. I hired a photographer and had a photoshoot of me doing yoga poses. I then took the art and photos and created a website.

I paid a graphic designer to design fliers that I wanted to pass out to promote the business. I had a launch where I offered free BUTI yoga for a week to get people in the door but then I quickly realized that fitness was a hard business because people were not consistent or motivated and that I would need to find something to do to cover my bases in addition to my yoga business to be able to pay my bills and provide for myself. I had to take a step back and reflect on why I decided to go to yoga teacher training and become a yoga teacher in the first place. I didn't do it because I thought I could make a bunch of money off of yoga, I did it because I wanted brown people that looked like to me to see more people that looked like them doing yoga. I wanted to influence them to eat better and live healthier lifestyles and perhaps try yoga and that it's not only for white people as many brown people assume because that's all they see in mass media.

    I was supposed to go to Clark Atlanta University's homecoming weekend to party with my friends in Atlanta but I decided to stay in Dallas and send resumes instead. Sometimes you have to make those hard decisions to sit out social activities that you may really want to do in order to take care of business that is necessary to help yourself. No one else is going to do it for you. Not your friends you are turning up with or the person you are dating. You have to make sacrifices for yourself to keep your life in order. One company that I sent my resume to responded to my e-mail within 12 hours of me sending it. It was for a children's school uniform designer posting on indeed.com that said the job was in Ft. Worth, Texas. A friend who knew I was looking for work sent it to me and a friend of hers sent it to someone she knew.

    When the company contacted me they said they wanted to schedule a phone interview with me but that it would have to be late at night my time and early in the morning their time because they were in Nairobi, Kenya. Once I had the phone interview the woman said that she had no idea why the job was listed as being located in Ft. Worth as the company has nothing to do with Texas at all. They needed someone that could freelance work from home and not even report in to an office considering they were located in Africa. I continued on with the interview process of sending samples of my work while they checked references, etc. A few weeks later the woman said they definitely wanted to bring me on but needed to get an approval from the CEO.

Right before Thanksgiving I received a call from a friend who was affiliated with the major retailer I had recently been laid off from and she asked me if I'd be interested in freelancing at the company in the women's active division because someone quit and they needed someone to cover that position while they searched for her replacement. Of course I said yes and she had me send my resume to the Sr. designer of that team. For the next month nothing really happened with anything. There were serious ice storms in Dallas so the retailer's office was closed often so I had no idea when and if they wanted me to start freelancing. My yoga business was very slow due to the weather as well and I was still waiting for the company in Africa to let me know what the CEO decided. During this time, I had an overwhelming feeling that I was experiencing the calm before the storm. It really felt like everything was chill and nothing was happening or moving but that God was doing this on purpose because there would come a time when I would be very busy again and not have a minute to breathe or think clearly. This feeling wasn't new to me because I remembered feeling it before that's why I was able to pinpoint exactly what I felt. Finally, the week before Christmas someone from H.R. at the major retailer reached out to me to see if I could start freelancing the next day. Of course I said 'yes' and went in and started working the next day. Friday of that same week the woman from the company in Africa reached out to me and said the CEO finally approved me to join the team as a freelancer designing and manufacturing school uniforms for all 352 of their schools in the slums throughout Kenya and for the schools they would soon be opening in other African countries and India.

As a result, I started 2014 with two freelance jobs and my business teaching BUTI Yoga. I was very busy. I prayed for one job in order to give me money to cover my bases while I worked to grow my yoga business and instead God blessed me with two opportunities that started at the same time. God is too good and when you let go and let his plan manifest this is the type of blessings you receive. During that year there were times that I got extremely overwhelmed with so much on my plate so I would outsource some of the work I needed to do for the uniforms and pay other freelancers to help me. I ended up going to Africa to fit the kids in the samples and then fly to India to work with the factory on the fit samples. Once the factory revised the samples I took them back to Africa, fit the children for the second time and then caught a flight back to the Dallas without anyone knowing where I was except close friends and family. I flew to Africa again to fit the kids for the last time without anyone knowing where I was once more in 2015 and as a result the uniforms finally went into production and the kids now are wearing their uniforms that I designed and manufactured for them.

I have since accepted a full time position back at the major retailer I was laid off from designing the women's private label active wear line. Which is super ironic considering I was laid off, became a yoga teacher and now design for the same company that I was laid off from in the active wear line. As a result of the work I did on the uniforms I have started a design consulting firm called Dream Design Group where the purpose is to provide people that have a vision but don't know how to get it accomplished a way to bring that dream to reality. My goal is to get DDG up and running to the point that I am able to quit my job and solely focus on my business and servicing my clients. I have hired a business coach to help me in the process and am looking forward to the amazing things God has planned for me in the future.

As a result, I hope you remember to always keep God first and keep faith over fear. God didn't put you here to worry, he carries those burdens for us. Then put yourself after God by making sure you are taking full care of yourself in all ways, body, mind and soul. Remember there will be many companies but only one you so do what you have to do to maintain your health by eating right, getting enough sleep, working out and finding ways to feed your soul and keep you peaceful and stress free. No matter how many hours you put in you can be let go at anytime so always be prepared, never get to comfortable. Keep some money saved in the bank, and live within your means. Stay focused on your goals by setting clear intentions then sit back and watch amazing miracles come to your life.

Susan Higgins is a fashion designer, yoga teacher, entrepreneur, lover of people, and now author living in Dallas, TX but originally born and raised in Rochester, NY. Susan was raised by two black hippies which is where she developed such an open mind, fearless spirit and willingness to carry out a conversation with anyone with ease and comfort. They taught her that no human is better than the next therefore never look down on anyone, you never know who you can learn from.

Workbook: Design

Companies use a vision statement to define who they are and what they will be in the future; it is the first step in creating a visual plan for yourself. As we women begin to put on the many hats required in our lives ranging from employee to mother, we often lose sight of us. Creating a personal vision statement will help you to remember and reclaim who you want to be, your passions, what you value, your motivators, and goals. Take your time and create a 1-2 sentence statement that will assist you on this journey in Designing Your Life!

Questions to assist you as you create your vision statement:
 + What are your beliefs and values?
 + What are your priorities?
 + What are the things you enjoy doing most?
 + What excites you? Fulfills you?
 + Where do you want to be in 3-5 years?

Vision Statement.

_____
_____
_____
_____
_____
_____
_____
_____

_____

Having a difficult time discovering your passion? Ask yourself the following:

If time, money, or family were not a factor, what would you be doing with your life?

What do you feel is stopping you from leaping into your passion?

Prayer

"Prayer is when you talk to God.
Meditation is when you listen to God."

-Unkonwn

Power, Perks, and Purpose of Prayer!

"Lord, just let me get my babies to school safely! I promise I will go straight to the hospital afterwards. Help me Lord!" This is what I cried out to the Lord on March 26, 2013 as I felt like my head was going to explode, my left side going numb, and like I was going to blackout. I hadn't prayed this hard in a long time, but I knew something serious was happening that would require the miracle of God.

I guess you are wondering, why I hadn't prayed in so long? Well, I'm glad you asked. You see, I was superwoman (in my own mind). I didn't need help from anyone, not even my Heavenly Father. I survived being abandoned by my son's father when my son was only three months old. Not to mention, I obtained my master's degree, bought a house and two vehicles as a single mom. That hasn't convinced you that I was "superwoman" yet? Well, when I married, it was because I wanted companionship, not because I needed him. I worked overtime, cooked, cleaned, paid bills, took care of the children and dealt with the trials of life by myself. Hubby was just there for decoration (Ha!). I had it going on (or so I thought). I was so busy trying to uphold my superwoman title, I neglected my prayer life. Now don't get me wrong, I grew up in church, directed and sang in choirs, was a youth leader etc. Prayer was a major part of my life in my early years. It's just as I grew older, I began to lean on my own strength and not God.

Now that you have a bit of history about me, let's get back to this particular day in 2013. I was home alone with my 7 and 1-year old children and was awakened by the worst headache I had ever experienced in my life. Although I was feeling faint, I was able to get my children up and ready for school. I didn't want them to have to endure seeing their mommy pass out, so I begin to pray to the Lord with all my might asking that He would be gracious enough to let me get my children to school safely. I was feeling pretty bad, but for goodness sake, I was only 34 years old which was surely too young to be having a stroke or heart attack. I decided it couldn't be too serious, and more than likely I just needed some rest.

So, I proceeded to take my children to school and drive myself to the hospital. After dropping my babies off, I began to feel my left arm going numb. I looked in the mirror and my mouth was starting to twist. The seriousness of my condition hit me hard and I became fearful. I called up the woman I knew could get a prayer through, my momma. As I tried to tell her I felt as though I was having a stroke, I became almost completely immobile on my left side and had to quickly pull over. My speech was no longer understandable, so I couldn't tell my mom where I was so that she could come get me. Good ole Debbie Ann (momma) knew exactly what to do; she started to intercede for me. She said she was hanging up the phone and I needed to try to call 911. When I managed to call 911, the dispatcher told me to try my best to blow the horn to get someone's attention because they couldn't understand me. I gathered enough strength to do so and soon after I heard a gentleman (my angel) telling me he was calling 911 and would stay with me until they arrived. He told me everything was going to be alright and for the moment, I somehow believed him.

About 2 minutes later I heard sirens. Yes, 2 minutes! Let me tell you how good God is, even in the midst of a storm. I had somehow pulled over less than one block from a fire/EMT station. Moving and speaking felt impossible, but I could hear everything going on around me. Only one thought was going through my mind over and over, "I shall not die, but live to declare the works of the Lord." The EMT declared I had signs of a stroke, so they immediately retrieved me out of the car and put me into the ambulance. He told me we were heading to Memorial Hermann Hospital's stroke center and we'd be there in about 15-minutes. I was starting to feel a little better and could finally speak again (my prayers were already working), though it was a bit slurred. I told the nice young man to turn around and take me back to my car because that 15-minute drive would cost me $15,000(I was kind of serious). He laughed and said my blood pressure was decreasing, but still way too elevated to not rush me to the hospital.

Upon my arrival at the hospital I was immediately taken to get a CAT scan. The CAT scan went by quickly and when I was done I told the technician that I had to use the restroom. He asked me if I was sure I can go by myself. Well, you know how "Superwoman" replied. Of course I could go by myself, I didn't need any help. I attempted to get off the hospital bed and walk myself to the restroom and found myself face down on the floor. Everyone came running over and the nurse reprimanded the technician for letting me get out of the bed by myself after possibly having a stroke. It was determined that I had lost mobility on my left side and I shouldn't try to walk by myself. Was this really happening to me? Why? While lying in the hospital bed, after falling onto the floor flat on my face, the reality of my situation became evident. I was indeed NOT superwoman, I needed help. I began crying uncontrollably and asking God to forgive me for neglecting Him and to please hear my prayer and heal my body. (Don't we tend to pray really hard in the midst of trouble, but other times prayer takes place only if we have time in our busy lives? Or is that just me?)

As I laid there crying, my husband walked in with a worried look on his face. He told me he had spoken with the doctor and the doctor was unsure of the long term effects from the stroke and would have to run further tests. The doctor came in soon after and told us according to the CAT scan I definitely had a stroke and we needed to decide immediately rather or not we wanted to do a procedure that reverses the effects of a stroke but has the side effects of: hemorrhaging in the brain that can cause unconsciousness or death, life threatening swelling, or rupture of the heart. So, basically I would either get 100 percent better or die. My husband looked at the doctor and told him we needed to discuss this and pray about it. (Did my husband really say pray about it? God was already working a miracle.) My husband (just as I) did not take the issues/troubles he faced to the Lord in prayer (which caused a lot of issues in our marriage. But, that's another story), so it was surprising to me that he immediately wanted to pray. The doctor warned that we only had a small window of time to reverse the stroke effects and we would have to think fast. He walked out and my husband began to pray, "God I'm afraid. I don't want to lose my wife. We need you to help us make this decision. I'd be lost without her."

Other than praying over our food I had never heard him pray before and it sure felt good to hear him tell God he needed Him and couldn't live without me. When we finished praying, my husband looked at me and said he didn't think I should do the stroke reversal procedure, but would support any decision I made. I was so relieved because we were on one accord. I didn't want to risk losing my life. The doctor walked in and we informed him that we had faith in our hearts that God would heal me and that we were declining the procedure. He looked shocked, but didn't press the issue. I don't think he understood just how awesome the God we serve is. I didn't know how long I would be unable to walk, but I did know that everything happens for a reason and all things work together for the good of those who love Him. (Roman 8:28).

Soon after my mom, dad and other family members came in and we all grabbed hands and begin to pray for God's divine healing. God made His presence known in that hospital room and I could feel my spirit begin to lift and felt comforted. I was admitted into the hospital and the doctors and nurses did what they could to make me feel comfortable and help me through my journey of recovery. If I told you I had faith the entire time and totally believed I would have a full recovery, I'd be kidding you and myself. I had many moments when my prayer was, "Why did this happen to me? Have I really been that bad of a person? Did I displease you that much, Lord? Why me?" But, as I read my Word more, listened to the Word of God on TV and started to pray a prayer of thanksgiving for God's grace and mercy (I was still alive!) my faith began to increase. After just 4 days of physical therapy, rest, a lot of care and prayer I was able to leave the hospital. Although I was walking on a cane, I had a lot more mobility than I had when I first arrived at the hospital. The doctors were amazed that I was in good spirits, laughing, and optimistic about my recovery. They just didn't know I had started to increase my praying which made my relationship with God stronger and I knew what God was going to do.

Returning back to my regular routine at home was very difficult because I had become accustomed to doing everything myself without asking for any help. I would be in the middle of cooking a meal and I'd have to ask my husband to bring me a chair to sit down because I had become weak and could no longer stand. Many evenings my husband had to pick me up and carry me to bed or help me shower because I didn't have the strength to stand on my own. Now, this all may sound so devastating. But God knew what He was doing. I was learning that it did not hurt to ask for help. I was learning that I could indeed count on my husband. At the same time my husband was learning how to serve and help out around the house. He was building a stronger relationship with the kids because they had to ask daddy to do a lot for them. And we were building a stronger marriage because we spent so much time together. The saying, "the family that prays together stays together" is a statement that I truly believe in now. My marriage and family was in a rocky place before I had a stroke. My marriage was leading towards that ugly road, divorce. But, as we prayed together for healing and peace and comfort, God brought us closer together. My husband began to feel needed and I began to realize how much I did need him to be the head of our household. My children were able to see how prayer and faith was so important. Didn't I tell you that all things work together for the good?

Although I didn't understand in the beginning why I was going through having a stroke, each day I prayed I felt stronger and my relationship with and faith in God grew stronger. Each time my husband carried me to bed because I was too weak to walk, I could feel our relationship grow stronger. I changed my lifestyle. I started to eat healthier, worked less hours, and stopped stressing over things I had no control over. Within 4 months I was walking without a cane, had a stronger relationship with God and the help from my husband that I should have asked for in the beginning. I now know that I am NOT "superwoman." I must manage stress, slow down, take care of myself, and ask for help in order to eliminate the possibility of having another stroke.

Why this long drawn out testimony? Good question. I want you to understand there is power, perks and purpose in prayer. I don't want you to wait until something tragic happens to begin praying. Prayer is as essential as breathing. Don't you breathe every day? Then, you should pray daily. Why is it important to pray daily? Well, glad you asked another great question.

1. God's Word Calls Us to Pray
God has commanded us to pray. If we are to be

obedient to His will, then prayer must be part of our life in Him. Prayer is an act of obedience. God calls us to pray and we must respond.

2. Jesus Prayed Regularly

As Christians we strive to be more like Jesus Christ. WWJD (what would Jesus do), Pray.

3. Prayer is How We Communicate with God

Prayer allows us to worship and praise the Lord and allows us to offer confession of our sins, which should lead to our genuine repentance. Prayer also gives us the opportunity to present our requests to God. Prayer is not just about asking for God's blessings, (though we are welcome to do so)but it is about communication with the living God. Without communication, relationships fall apart. So, too, our relationship with God suffers when we do not communicate with Him.

4. Prayer Gives Us Power Over Evil

"For our struggle is not against flesh and blood, but against the rulers, against the authorities, against the powers of this dark world and against the spiritual forces of evil in the heavenly realms" (Ephesians 6:12). But in prayer even the physically weak can become strong in the spiritual realm. As such, we can call upon God to grant us power over evil.

5. Prayer Keeps Us Humble Before God

Humility is a virtue God desires in us. Prayer reminds us that we are not in control, but God is, thus keeping us from pride.

6. Prayer Grants Us the Privilege of Experiencing God

Through prayer we obtain an experiential basis for our faith. We do not ignore the intellect or reasons for faith, but prayer makes our experience of God real on an emotional level. We were made to function best, emotionally, in a prayerful relationship with God.

7. Answered Prayer is a Potential Witness
If our prayer is answered, it can serve as a potential witness for those who doubt.

8. Prayer Strengthens the Bonds Between Believers
Prayer not only strengthens our relationship with God, but when we pray with other believers, prayer also strengthens the bonds between fellow Christians.

9. Prayer Can Succeed Where Other Means Have Failed
There are times when sincere prayer must be offered in order to succeed at something where other means have failed. Prayer should not be a last resort, but our first response. Neglecting prayer results in weakness and defeat. I've found the answer in prayer; I'll tell it everywhere; I know what prayer can do. Prayer has changed my life and I hope you allow it to change yours too.

Priscilla Green is a passionate teacher, counselor, and motivational speaker. In addition, she is a mother of three beautiful children (Karen 13, Elijah 10, and RaiAnna 4), and the wife of an extraordinary husband. She has spent the last 10 years of her professional career teaching, counseling and encouraging elementary aged students to be the best they can be. In recent years, she has encouraged women to have a deeper relationship with God and stronger prayer life. As a motivational speaker, Priscilla addresses women groups, social groups, and youth groups with the hopes of using her testimony to reach many for the Kingdom of God.

Finding God in Myself (and I Loved Her)

"Everyday someone tells me I'm beautiful, one day I hope to believe it." I remember writing this in my journal at twenty-something growing up in Harlem. I moved there right after college and fell in love with its layered vibrancy. The nature of Harlem has that good grandma love; whips you when you act a fool but kisses the tears dry when she's through. I soaked up that Harlem love alongside the many brown faces I encountered each day. These faces, pouring love into my life, kept my spirits lifted as I battled myself silently, often losing.

I never felt like I struggled with self-esteem issues until I look back at that time. I was new to New York, new to the "real world" as a first-time adult and new to the entertainment industry that I was desperate to belong. The only things that kept me grounded were my faith in God and my hunger to "live my dreams". Moving to New York and working in the TV industry (BET at the time) was a part of that dream and I had finally accomplished it! But shortly after, I was SO insecure with myself. There was so much competition: so many people who were "better," smarter, more attractive, more connected, more established, more financially stable….it goes on and on. I began a habit of constantly doubting myself and not being content. This double-mindedness clouded my judgments and made everything confusing. I wasn't clear about the direction of my life anymore and ended up constantly feeling disappointed.

Later, one of my mentors would say "compare and despair." A phrase I continue to use when I find myself looking at others more than I look at myself. I was living in despair – feeling hopeless, tired and needing to look around for validation and not within.

The clearest example of this desperate time

was when I left BET, and the television industry, to pursue my acting career - a dream of mine since I was 5 years old. I remember being on my production sets and watching the actors play (most of the time critiquing them), and discovering the truth…I missed it.

I had been acting on stage and on camera since I was a child. I went to college (on scholarship) for my BFA in acting. I didn't know what life was without it. But when pressure got tough and my creativity was shorted, I turned to television production as my new artistic expression. And I loved it, but it was a different kind of love…the love of creative control, and ultimately I chose production over acting.

Since making that choice, I still wanted to act. So I did. And I got busy! Headshots, resumes, agents, auditions. I booked commercials, print editorials and films. I was focused…until I wasn't. One afternoon, I met this charming young lady at an audition who unconsciously altered my path in acting. Her name was Sparkle.

Sparkle and I instantly became friends and she was the type of girl that lights up a room (hence her name). She was super talented and everyone liked her. She was hard working, God-fearing and beautiful…just dripping in success, even though we were on the same level in our acting careers. When we joined the same acting class, she murdered every scene. She was the instructor's (and the class) favorite. She was a natural star and this made me insecure.

I started to compare my skills, my looks, even my spirituality with her. It seemed she had me beat in every area. I felt like a failure and a fraud. How can I compete with her? Who am I to think I can possibly be chosen in a role over her? I'm not good enough!

And I believed me. So I stopped pursuing

acting and years later, Sparkle booked a leading role on one of the top TV shows while I watched.

This experience (along with many others) taught me the power of my thoughts. I can think my way to success or think my way to failure and the major difference in these thoughts reflect in my level of self-love. When I feel loved, beautiful and confident, my thought life is positive, fruitful and high frequency energy, which causes me to make better life choices that lead to personal fulfillment and happiness. When I feel unappreciated, disrespected and confused, my thought life is negative, doubtful and low vibrational energy causing hopelessness and regrettable choice making.

It should be noted that the feelings or emotions associated with these thoughts can be the cause or effect of your thinking. So you can have negative thoughts and afterwards feel low or you can feel low then afterwards have the negative thoughts. Thoughts and emotions are closely correlated in vibrational energy.

Energy Coach, Melody Fletcher, states "Everything is energy. Everything we can see, hear, touch, taste and smell is made of different wavelengths vibrating at different frequencies. Our brain is like a translator that has the ability to interpret these frequencies into what we perceive to be our physical reality. Every time you think a thought, you send out that thought's specific vibration. If a thought makes you feel good, if it's a "positive" thought, it is vibrating at a higher frequency. If a thought makes you feel bad, if it's a "negative" thought, it's vibrating at a lower frequency. So, "I hate you" has a much lower frequency than "I love you", for example.

It took me about two years to fully embrace the concept of recognizing and maintaining healthy thoughts. I knew that I had to change and WHY I needed to, but it was difficult to know HOW to change. I went to church, seminars, hired a life coach, exercised but all of these external resources gave me a temporary fix- a shot of inspiration- but didn't sink deep enough to actually create change.

The answer was in me.

I started learning ways to be with myself, so that I can connect with my soul, my spirit and God. Creating time that can be dedicated to my attention -MYSELF- was my first discovery to self-love. This me-time became the most important part of my day, not only to get to know myself more but to connect with God who is inside of me.

Author and wellness coach, Fawne Hanson, says "Taking some 'me' time can help you avoid irritability and enable you to control your emotions. A little time for yourself refreshes and re-energizes you. 'Me' time also builds your self-esteem over time, as you come to realize that you are important and deserve to give time to yourself. Other benefits include the ability to sleep better, less fatigue, depression and anxiety, greater resistance to sickness, and less tension. Indirectly, taking time for yourself may also improve your interpersonal and business relationships, making you a better partner, parent, or employee."

As I challenged myself to honor this time, I began to honor me. I couldn't remember the last time that I turned off everything to just be. For the first time, I was my own priority. Not my family, friends, boyfriend, work, social media, email…nope, it was all about me! I gave away my time to too many things that are less important than me, it was time to give myself the love and attention I craved.

I started with setting aside 20 minutes each morning to sit in silence and have internal connection. It didn't start off as meditating; I was just closing my eyes and thinking about what made me happy and what I desired in my life. The more I focused on myself, the more appreciation I felt. I was being intimate with my inner spirit- the Spirit of God- and I discovered so much love. Putting that 20 minutes in each morning automatically boosted my self-worth. I loved it so much that the 20 minutes evolved into an hour. I called it my POWER HOUR.

POWER HOUR looked like this:

Wake up at 6:00am: This was already a challenge because at the time, I was working from home and didn't necessarily have to be anywhere by any specific time. But I knew how my mornings can easily get filled with distractions, so I made the choice to be up early enough to focus on my time without any disruptions.

I like the way best-selling author Gary Keller puts it, "Getting up early is a decision. It's usually not an easy decision, which is why people who rise early tend to feel that they have a better sense of control. Battling temptation and winning at the brink of dawn sets the tone for the entire day, and typically that means feeling like you can take on whatever else life throws at you."

Early risers are usually more energized, focused and productive because they have more time and discipline in the day as a result. I also had to make decisions about how I spend my time the night before. If I wanted to wake up early, I had to go to sleep early. Giving myself a bed time helped me make the transition to being an early riser easier.

6:00am -6:10am: Prayer. Prayer changes everything. My late Grandma Suber taught me how to pray and it's been my comfort and joy ever since. I spend this time focused on the people and areas in my life that I want to give support and love to. I envision healing, opportunities, safety, clarity and trust God with my deepest insecurities and pain. The energy exchange between me and God in this moment allows me to release any excess worries that can taunt my mind.

"Prayer at its highest is a two-way conversation and for me the most important part is listening to God's replies." — Frank C. Laubach

I pray in many ways, sometimes internally, sometimes out loud. I write my prayers too. The purpose of prayer is to create a special space to surrender your cares to God and listen for gentle guidance.

6:10am - 6:30am: Inspirational Reading/Journaling. I always have a book (or two!) to read, even if it's the Bible. Starting your morning with a positive word or affirmation always steers the mind in the right direction. This is the set-up for the step-up in your day. When you get your mind in a safe happy space to recognize how great you are, it expands in that space causing great rewards in your energy, thoughts and experiences.

I've been learning about the effect that thoughts, behaviors and exposure to certain external sources affect your health and well-being. One of the ways to be happier is to focus in things that make you feel inspired and uplifted. A good read or affirmation in the morning can put a smile on your day. Happiness Expert, Shawn Anchor, explains, "When our brains constantly scan for and focus on the positive, we profit from three of the most important tools available to us: happiness, gratitude, and optimism. The role happiness plays should be obvious—the more you pick up on the positive around you, the better you'll feel."

After reading for 15 minutes, take 5 minutes to do some soul writing - thoughtless writing that comes from within with emotion, honesty and passion. I've written about my past, about dreams, about my future, the new boy I'm crushing on - anything that was on my heart has filled pages of journals throughout the years.

Life Coach, Elyse Santilli, describes this process of soul writing as "open and complete honesty. It is not like writing a diary where you may be tempted to recount events in a certain skewed or selective way that suits you best. No one is ever going to read this. You don't need to put a spin on things, or hold back how you really feel, however 'crazy' you may think it sounds. Don't be afraid of being raw and vulnerable."

6:30am -6:40am: Stretch. Before I got serious about yoga, I used this time to do basic stretching to wake up my body. While I would stretch, I would pray over my body for health and strength while giving thanks for all the blessings my body gave me. A basic sun salutation is a good stretching series but letting your body lead you to its needs is best.

Fitness expert, Sarah Dreifke, writes, "The most established and obvious benefit of stretching is to help improve flexibility and range of motion. A lack of flexibility can cause movement to become slower and less fluid, making an individual more susceptible to muscle strains. Everyone has stress. A buildup of stress causes your muscles to contract, becoming tense. This tension can go on to have a negative impact on just about every part of your body. Like all types of exercise, flexibility exercises like stretching have powerful stress-busting abilities. Spending just a short amount of time (10-15 minutes) stretching each day can help calm the mind, providing a mental break and giving your body a chance to recharge."

6:40 am - 7:00am: Meditation. Meditation saved my life. Seriously. Meditation is my time to love myself deeply. It's about bringing your attention within and letting go of stress, anxiety and negativity. It's everything and nothing. It's the fullness of life. Breath.

Twenty minutes of my hour is spent in stillness… eyes clothes, deep breathing. Thoughts come and go, my mantra comes and goes but I just sit and breathe and feel the love.

I deepened my meditation practice with an organization called The Art of Living. This foundation taught me how to deepen my meditation experience with breathing exercises. When they describe meditation, they explain, "The rest in meditation is deeper than the deepest sleep that you can ever have. When the mind becomes free from agitation, is calm and serene and at peace, meditation happens. The benefits of meditation are manifold. It is an essential practice for mental hygiene. A calm mind, good concentration, clarity of perception, improvement in communication, blossoming of skills and talents, an unshakeable inner strength, healing, the ability to connect to an inner source of energy, relaxation, rejuvenation, and good luck are all natural results of meditating regularly."

Meditation made me realize how beautifully powerful I am and how great it is to be alive!

Through my **POWER HOUR**, I began to regain the love and confidence I haven't felt since I was a child. I discovered how connected I am to God and the Universe. I realized my potential and the fullness of my life. I stopped chasing external fulfillment and appreciated the power within me. I found God in myself.

And I loved her.

Once I experienced this love, God opened the world to me from the inside out. I began to reconnect with my purpose of inspiring young women through media and moved to Los Angeles to pursue it. Soon after moving, I started working for an inspirational media company that was once on my vision board – the Oprah Winfrey Network. While in LA, I've traveled to five continents (including Africa) doing spiritual and social services and I organized a support group of women who constantly experience miracles. I'm currently building a beautiful brand on self-love, becoming a yoga teacher, and I'm back to acting :)

My new experiences are due to the power of self-love, a love that truly connects you to God because God is in you. The best summary of this power comes from one of my greatest spiritual teachers, Lauryn Hill, in the song 'The Miseduction of Lauryn Hill': And deep in my heart/ the answer it was in me/ and I made up my mind/ to define my own destiny I found my answer. God – in me.

Samora is a free-spirited creative, always looking for the joke and the adventure! A New Orleans native who was raised in equal parts Charlotte and New York – she now resides in Los Angeles where she works at the Oprah Winfrey Network while teaching yoga and developing her lifestyle media brand.
She is a friend of God, she likes to create impromptu photo shoots and she can't stop traveling!

Sweet Hour of Prayer

"Sweet hour of prayer, sweet hour of prayer. That calls me from a world of care. And bids me at my Father's throne. Makes all my wants and wishes known. In seasons of distress and grief. My soul has often found relief. And oft escape the tempters snare. By thy return sweet hour of prayer."

I never understood why on God's green earth Pastor Coleman made us sing that song EVERY Sunday before alter call. I think I was in middle school the first time I heard it and in my thirties the first time I understood its relevance in the connection between the importance of prayer and its power. I don't know why the song popped in my head when it did, other than God knowing I needed Him most. My son was away and I was lying in bed contemplating suicide. I was over the feeling of another failed opportunity at happiness (as I saw it) as a result of my horrible attitude. I thought about all the years of failed attempts at dating, each ending with me acting in a manner than left me feeling embarrassed at my actions for at least 24 hours. Now, I had no issue being single, but I had issue with the fact that EACH failed relationship, was my fault.

The details behind the failures didn't matter this time, it was finally the "why" that depressed me so much. By the "why" I mean the reason I felt it appropriate to behave so irrationally towards people I claimed to care about. Now, I will not go into depths on my why. That is not the goal of this story as we each have our own whys that brought us to this point. What I will say is each of our "whys" are relevant and deserve to be seen and heard, and that, does not always happen. Many times we carry these whys with us for years, allowing them to fester and grow beneath our surface, many times unbeknownst to us. It is not until we hit a low point of wanting to die that we begin to unearth how we got here. For many, this is when the actual suicide occurs, if you ask me. For me, this is when God reminded me of how sweet an hour of prayer could be.

Realizing why I was so angry then led me to thinking about how I treated others as a result of my pain. This is probably the second reason why people commit suicide. Again, none of this is research proven, just my personal reflections from the bottom. But when we take the time to think about how we have treated loved ones, family, friends, significant others, and, most importantly to me, my child- it can mess you up! Thinking back on things I have said to people, all I can say is, I am blessed to be alive.

It is embarrassing and shameful when I think back on my actions over the past ten years, especially with my level of education and professional accomplishments. I even had more than one man say to me "for you to be so educated, how can you be so crazy?" which should have been a clear indication that I had an issue, but I took it as a challenge to live up to the word crazy and act in an even more irrational manner. I've learned that we all have our "thing": our way of treating people or ourselves when we are hurt or upset. This ranges from drinking, drugs, and binge eating, to cutting, violence, or for me cussing people the hell out. I know you may be thinking, "cussing someone out isn't that bad" and this is where I wish the men I dated could contribute excerpts into the craziness that is angry me.

When I am angry, it's almost as if I black out for a period of one to three days. During this period, a floodgate of the nastiest things I could muster up would be said to men I had just claimed to care about hours before. I have talked about deceased parents, kids, finances, jobs, circumstances, vehicles, attire, I mean if there was a way to insult it- I found it. I attempted to emasculate men through words, not sure what reaction I was hoping for other than to push them away for not "loving" me, as sad as it may sound. Again, this is something I have known that I did for years and got quite good at it, if you ask me. However, I finally reached a point of being tired, of wondering if I really was crazy, and of being ashamed to look someone in the eyes because of how I treated them.

As a parent, my anger was less subtle, but still there. Unfortunately, the people who live with us or that we communicate with are typically the ones that have to deal with our issues first-hand. Looking back, I fussed longer than necessary, yelled when I could have talked, and had expectations that were not always fit for a child. Recognizing this added to my hurt because I believe that since children do not ask to be born, they deserve nothing but the best. Treating a child in a damaging manner leads to what are often referred to as generational curses; we have to be the generation to stop the cycle.

***

I laid in bed crying for about three days before the song came into my head. During this time, I thought about praying; I probably even mumbled "Lord help me" between changing snot rags. I even went through the motion of listening while my prayer partner did her absolute best to life my spirits by praying over me, but I never PRAYED. Many people have their own idea what it means to pray. Some people move their lips and mouth the words to not disturb the peace, others reflect deeply on the mediations of their heart, and there are others who view meditation as a form of prayer. For me, prayer means opening your mouth and letting your voice articulate the petitions of your heart, almost like talking to your best friend, matter-of-fact, just like it.

When I finally accepted the fact that I needed to pray, I cried at the thought of the things I needed to bring through my lips. The many apologies for the things I have said with the sole purpose of hurting others, the cries of prayers for peace that passes understanding, and the ability to heal knowing that I have to forgive someone who will never apologize. This is where I enter my life isn't fair rant. It is NOT fair that many of us in this world have to find a way to forgive someone who will NEVER acknowledge they wronged us to provide a respectful apology. There are so many scenarios in life where this takes place from childhood abuse, to witnessing things at home that you think are normal only to find out they are socially unacceptable, to a parent choosing not to parent all of which equally damaging and worthy of recognition. Many times all we want is to feel seen, heard, respected, acknowledged, recognized. Unfortunately, life isn't fair and we, instead, must turn to prayer to find peace in our pain.

    I am not writing this as a how-to manual on prayer. What I am hoping to accomplish is guiding others how to open themselves up in a way that allows them to experience the peace prayer brings in a way they (you) have not before. When we simply go through what we think are the motions of praying, we oftentimes, find ourselves reciting what we think should be said; we ask for the typical blessings over our family, friends, and finances, and maybe a quick "forgive me of my sins". But when you really learn to TALK to God, to open yourself up and become vulnerable in His presence, a change can occur.

When you pray:
- Pray for healing- ask God to help you move past this place of darkness
- Pray for forgiveness- ask God to forgive you for those you hurt through your pain and depression
- Prayer for purpose- ask God to show you why he created you
- Pray for discernment- ask God to show you everything that will take you away from your purpose

Healing. Praying for healing will be difficult if you have not come to terms with what you believe has damaged you. For some, this may require counseling, which I am a strong advocate of. I think talking to a knowledgeable individual, who will listen without bias, and provide perspective, is healthy. Again, I will not divulge into what I needed healing from but I can say telling God how I no longer wanted to feel as a result was cleansing. Tell God what you are sick and tired of, literally. Ask God what you want to be pulled from and what you want to be moved to. Start speaking how you want to feel into existence as much as you declare what you will not go back to feeling life. Take time doing this, all the hurt did not happen in a matter of minutes, so asking God to move you past it will not either. Do not think of this as complaining or that by reflecting so heavily on the past that you are minimizing that God has done for you. In reality, you are opening yourself up to see more of what God has in store for you by getting those monkeys off your back that have held you down for so long.

Pray for forgiveness. I have never fully understood the concept of confession, however, I feel that this concept applies accurately in this scenario. While you are in your moment of prayer, open your mouth and apologize to the Lord for the ways in which you have sinned. I had to apologize for thinking I was worthy enough to speak so rudely to His children, for being so arrogant about my accomplishments and using them to belittle others who I felt were not on my level, for not being the type of parent I know I am capable of being, for not treating my temple as I should not only through sexual activity but not taking care of my health, for not being the type of friend I desire others to be, and so forth and so on. Yes, over the past ten years I had prayed for forgiveness for my sins on many occasions- this was the first time I really meant it. Meaning it means you have to be ready to follow this prayer up with change, which we will tackle in the next chapter, and for me is how this book was birthed. Using my pain to bless others is my way of showing the Lord, and prayerfully those I hurt, that I understand how wrong I was.

Asking for forgiveness was of special importance to me because I am a huge believer in the concept of karma: everything you do comes back to you. Many times when negative situations would occur, I would ask myself "what did I do to deserve this?" not reflecting on the hurtful things I had said and done to others putting bad karma into the universe. The Bible tells us that we reap what we sow (Galatians 6:7) so we cannot disrespect God's children, regardless of what we think they deserve, and benefit everything that God truly has in store for us. Once you ask for forgiveness, and really mean it, you are lifting a cloud of pre-destined bad luck from over you.

Pray for Purpose. Life is nothing without purpose. Purpose is what wakes us up in the morning and what drives us. It is that thing that without it, we would be incomplete. Not just our family or children, but something that makes us the unique individual that we are as a Christian. God did not just create us to walk this Earth, but to serve in some way, shape, or form. Doctors, teachers, entertainers, preachers, philanthropists, city workers all have purpose. Have you ever asked God what is yours? Or more importantly, do you know what it is but are afraid to live in it? God did not create us to be mediocre. We do not walk the Christian walk to roam lost but serve in our purpose to have life more abundantly (John 10:10). Ask God to show you how you were created to serve the world as His vessel. I promise having a purpose that includes service to others will give you a reason to live. I work in higher education and when I finished my prayer God told me to text a few of my students to make sure they were registered and ready for the upcoming semester. Their replies of gratitude that someone was concerned about their educational wellbeing made me start feeling like myself again because I was walking in God's path of purpose for me.

Pray for discernment. Google describes discernment in the Christian context as "perception in the absence of judgment with a view to obtaining spiritual direction and understanding" (2016). Just as there are individuals that we feel caused the situations that put us where we are mentally and emotionally, there are individuals and people that keep us there.
Asking for the gift of discernment allows you to see what needs to be removed from your life, what should be focused on, and in what order. This can be challenging when what we NEED to focus on conflicts with what we WANT to focus on. I want a relationship, to be married, to be one of those sickening people posting selfies and #MCM hashtags on social media but I am not ready due to my emotional baggage. Until I fully heal myself, I will continue to destroy relationships, and it took me praying for discernment to understand that God is not saying "no" but rather "not right now." here are more important things that I need to focus on, number one being my son, the other, my career. Ask God to show you where you are mismanaging yourself and to help you remove those things, or people, to make room for Him and what he desires of you. As you discover your purpose, it will be much easier to determine what/who must stay or go.

Notice that the definition of discernment

contains the caveat 'without judgment' meaning we must not look down on what we come up from. I will say that again: we must not look down on what we come up from. Once you move past your place of pain, you cannot look down on those who have yet to heal. You may disassociate yourself but never do so while elevating yourself and forgetting where you just came from.

80s babies will remember the time of the gospel music infomercials on BET where you could get all your gospel hits in one place (to be read in your best advertising voice). There was one in particular where an elderly woman sings the song 'In the Room.' The message within this song is that we must go into a place of isolation to talk to God; some now refer to this as a War Room. For me, it isn't a room, but a place in my house, my personal alter of sorts where I go to reveal myself to God. Whatever this place may be for you, find one and designate it as your place of prayer. Go to this place distraction free and be prepared to spend a good deal of time with God. My first real prayer of healing lasted almost thirty minutes. Not to criticize, but if you truly feel you are damaged and find yourself out of things to say to the Lord after five or ten minutes, you are not being honest with yourself or Him. As the song says, allow God to call you from your world of care and into His presence.

When my best friend is going through something that requires intimate time with God, she goes as far as shutting out as much of the outside world as possible. For her, this means no phone calls that do not relate to work or her kids and a break from social media so she can give her undivided attention to the Lord. If any of you reading this are extroverts like me, this can be painfully challenging; however, after trying it, I can say it is the best way to talk to AND receive God's message for you. You may be thinking that it is rude to ignore phone calls or that people may be offended if they do not hear from you for a week or two, but that will also be God's way of showing you who is really for you and who is not. Any friend that cannot accept you taking time to work on yourself, is not a friend, and this is one reason why praying for discernment is so important. Healing is no good if you go right back to the people or things that burdened your mind, body, and spirit for so many years.

My prayer for you is that after reading my story, and others without the book, you take time for yourself to talk to God and receive the many messages He has for your life.

Consuela Cooper, a self-proclaimed "nerd girl" resides in Houston, TX while completing her PhD in Education Leadership, Policy, and Change. Consuela prides herself on being a Christian who hopes to use her struggles through life to help other women. She understands the taboo of sexual abuse and depression held by so many Black families and hopes that by talking about these topics, lines of communication can be opened and healing may begin.

Workbook: Her

One of the most important things a woman can give herself is "me time"; time to get our nails done, read a good book, take a candle-lit bubble bath, or go for a peaceful walk through the park. Just as we need time to rejuvenate our minds and bodies we must take time to talk to God in a private place so we can not only make our concerns and desires known, but also be prepared to receive answers. Think of this time as rejuvenation for your soul. The popular movie War Room encourages us to create a space to do just that. Rather than providing a written exercise, we encourage our readers to take time to find a spot in their home that can be a designated place of prayer and meditation using the tips below:

+ Clear out a small space in a closet or corner

+ Make notes of your prayer requests or posts pictures of the individuals you are praying for

+ Get used to praying in a kneeled position; if kneeling isn't possible, use a chair that you can sit in for prayer

+ Keep your Bible near for those times God is ready to speak to you through His word

+ If you don't have a "room" that you can clear out, find a corner that you can use in the same manner

+ If praying is new to you, invest in a prayer journal or devotional book to assist you!

Remember, the key is carving out time for prayer and meditation. The busier you are, the more time you need to spend alone with God!

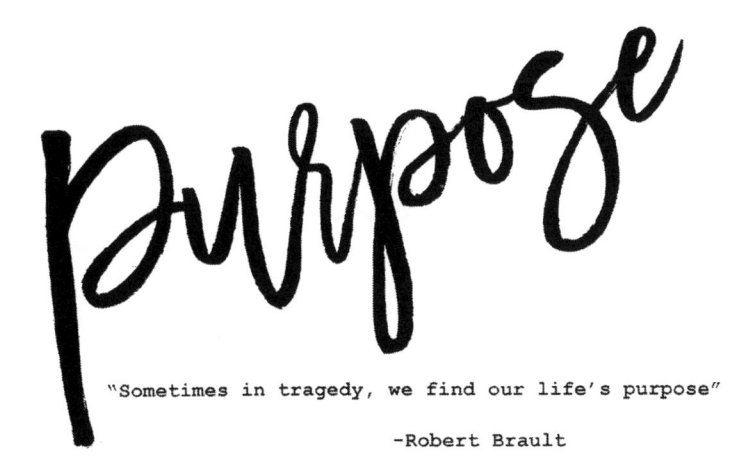

purpose

"Sometimes in tragedy, we find our life's purpose"

-Robert Brault

The Reality of Happiness

Every day I wake up tired or sometimes even exhausted. I roll around on the layers of blankets I arranged for us the night before and think about how I'd once again failed to make our place of rest a comfortable one. Not even the most plush blankets and pillows can replace my Queen sized memory foam mattress that is now in storage. Dre, my 3-year-old Godson, has been with me almost two years. I'd recently been given guardianship and although he gladly follows me wherever I go and sleeps where I lay him without question or complaint, I can't help but wonder if he's comfortable. We moved back to Texas only 5 months ago and are living with my mom in her one bedroom apartment. I haven't lived in Texas in five years so it's nice to be around family again. But, it's on mornings like these I wake up dreaming about better days. One of the first things on my list is to move back to New York and with my goal date just around the corner the pressure is on! I know this pressure... I've encountered it a time or two in previous situations. The difference in the pressure this time is the fact that I have a child with me and the risks I would have taken for myself long ago wouldn't exactly provide a consistently nurturing atmosphere for a child. This pressure is the pressure to get it right! Sometimes it feels like I'm being suffocated by my concerns. "Where will I work? Where will we live? What is the best school for Dre?" All of these things, a few others, and one other very important aspect concerning New York stick out in my mind. I'd previously lived in New York while attending the Stella Adler Studio of Acting and though I'd count it as a successful run, it wasn't easy by far. It was very rough at times. But it was in that rough space that I discovered a feeling I only thought I'd experienced before, happiness.

Let's hear it for New York

    I applied to the acting studio and was accepted very quickly. I was elated and maybe even almost in a state of disbelief that I was finally able to move to my beloved New York and study in the field I'd dedicated my entire existence to. I found a job almost immediately and because I worked in hospitality, wasn't moved by the fact that I was unable to secure a home before the move. I planned to use my employee rate from the hotel and move around the big city to whichever property offered the best rate for the night. Fool proof right? Well, not exactly. I purchased my one-way ticket and arrived in New York ready for whatever it threw my way. I attended the studio during the day, worked the night audit shift at the hotel, and still managed to execute my plan to move around the city to whichever hotel offered the best rate. My classes were great. I learned so much and met so many different people from all over the world. So many people extended help when they could in every sort of situation from studying to helping me pull my 50 lb. bags around and in/out of the subways. I was literally functioning on a dream and faith... working at night, school during the day, and the rest of the time on the subway to switch hotels, get showered, and preparing myself to do it all over again.

    I was a part of the New York hustle and bustle that up until then, I had only been able to see from afar. I loved it! But, I was exhausted! I was so drained… I felt like I wasn't excelling at my dreams but instead doing just enough to get by on whatever energy I had left. And if that wasn't bad enough, one day I realized that I was essentially wasting my money. I only spent an hour or two in the hotel changing and actually used more time in transit to get there. I was in need of basic essentials and finally decided to save time spent in transit and the money I was using on lodging by leaving my bags at work, showering where I could, and getting sleep or relaxing in a nearby subway or wherever the opportunity presented itself. I slept on my lunch breaks, on the subway, in Barnes & Noble, anywhere I felt safe. But the one place that really stood out for me was Starbucks! I was able to rest without feeling like I was in the way or bothering anyone. It became my go-to. When 7 am hit I said a few goodbyes and rushed out the door to get a power nap in before my first class at around 9:30 am. I started out ordering coffee, tea, or SOMETHING so that it appeared that I'd fallen asleep during my morning routine. But after a while, I didn't care. I'd walk in and go straight to my spot, get comfortable, and allow myself to fall asleep.

One day I chose a small wooden table at the top of a stair case and 30 minutes or so into my nap felt myself being moved and shaken. I woke up very disoriented and startled and for a while my eyes couldn't focus properly. I finally came to and realized that the tall silhouette in front of me was the manager. He said "Wake up! This isn't a place for sleeping so you need to either purchase something or leave...YOU CAN'T SLEEP HERE!" I could feel the stares from everyone around me... a room full of people that were just as taken aback as I was. I quickly gathered myself, my things and left shocked but surprisingly, unfazed. I headed up the street to my next destination and made my morning call to my Mom. Of course after hearing what had just happened she was very upset, worried, and even presented her case as to why I should leave New York. Armed with fact after fact about my time in New York she gave a speech as if it were the State of the Union Address. She went in! She rarely even stopped for a breath when finally, I interrupted. "Momma... I'm not leaving." A big part of me felt like I didn't have anything to go back to... I was raised by two parents that were addicted to Heroin and even though my mom had been clean for several years, I'd been exposed to some rough times. One of the things that was most cathartic for me in those years was my time on stage and after making it through still holding on to my dreams and at times because of my dreams, I was determined not to give up on them because things were a little difficult. After a deep breath, I continued "This is where I'm supposed to be and this is what I'm supposed to be doing. God is providing and protecting and, I'M HAPPY! And that makes it worth it..." It was almost as if I was sitting in on a conversation with my Mom and someone else. I was just as shocked at what I was saying as she was.

As I heard myself utter those words I allowed myself to feel how true it was and took comfort in how good it felt. I'd been faced with hurdle after hurdle. Clearing some with little effort... and barely making it over others with everything in me. In the midst of the race I had acquired strength, growth, and something else really special and rare... Happiness. So, I know advice from a free spirited rebel may not be extremely popular; but in the next few pages I'll share tips gained through different experiences and attempt to shine a light on the kind of happiness that has me packing my bags, welcoming a few risks, and heading for New York.

The Journey
"Whatever it is... let it be" -Jill Scott

I LOVE traveling. There's something about venturing into the unknown and leaving out with a fresh, new perspective. I've always been intrigued by trying new activities, different cultures and their cuisines, feeling a new texture, and, sometimes, smelling new fragrances. I'm the kind of traveler that likes to immerse myself into my surroundings so much that when I leave a piece of the culture is in me and a piece is, undoubtedly, left behind. I like to allow the moment to organize the journey... taking me wherever a breeze blows freely. So, with all of that in mind, you'd think I would be more prone to savor the curve balls life sometimes throws out. Right? Eh... not so much!

I will never forget my first week with Dre. It was a complete shock to my system! I've always loved kids and loved nurturing, teaching, and spoiling them. I was so excited that I would be able to help out full time and show a child a different kind of living by exposing him to anything that would make his imagination go bananas. My story about life in New York may not be any indication but, I love a good nap! I like to sleep late so the first morning he woke me up saying "Jamie... I'm hungry" I was almost insulted. At that moment I knew that I was in for a few life lessons. Anyone that has kids or has been around kids for an extended period of time knows that some days NOTHING goes as planned. When they have to use the bathroom it doesn't matter that you're in New Orleans walking through the French Quarter. You find a bathroom! Sometimes the meal that is usually complete in 20 minutes will take 45 minutes. You can make a schedule but you have to understand going in that it may not happen exactly that way. It makes no sense to get frustrated or upset with the inconsistencies during their growth. If you allow yourself to be upset by that, you'll always be upset.

I would love if everything in life could go the way I planned. Knowing that things can and will probably go off course sometimes affects my confidence and motivation to plan anything at all. But I've learned that trying to control the journey can be completely debilitating to the process. Just as with a child, we won't be able to truly nurture life by focusing so much on what isn't going as planned because it takes our attention off of how beautiful the journey is. We have to learn to appreciate the entire process and trust that every lesson it brings with it will ultimately add to our Happiness in some way. I've seen a quote for years that says "If you stumble make it a part of the dance" and that is exactly what this is all about. Embrace your journey and "whatever it is... let it be." Happiness will be there around a corner, peeking in the shadows... choose to see it.

The Happiest Life

Almost daily I log into my Instagram or Facebook account and see big, lavish celebrations for various reasons all over my timeline. You know the ones I'm talking about… the big, beautiful weddings, baby showers, and birthday parties with the best food, decorations, and activities. I am completely obsessed with event planning but personally I'm not usually the go all out type. But up until a few years ago I would begin preparations for a "big" birthday celebration. Every year! I'd look for the perfect place, the perfect outfit all the way down to the polish on my toes, and of course, there's the "guest list." I would create something in my mind that was so grand and would almost always be disappointed when the actual day came around. Finally, I decided to do something that made more sense for me on my birthday.

While visiting my second home, New Orleans, I began to think about the things that really make me happy. It didn't take very long for me to realize that a big piece of my happiness is found in making others happy so, I decided that I would celebrate my birthday by giving back. I arranged for a few of us to meet under a bridge in New Orleans that plays double duty as a bridge to the West bank of New Orleans and shelter for much of the homeless population. I showed up with enough ice cold water, hot dogs, and popsicles for nearly 80 people and we gladly passed out the items to the homeless and less fortunate population of New Orleans in bags that said "Thanks for Celebrating with me." We stood around for a little while talking, snapping pictures with my new friends, and receiving wishes for a Happy Birthday. It was the perfect day and I really felt as special as I'd always hoped and planned in prior years. Wow! I wasn't surprised that I enjoyed it as much as I was shocked that I hadn't thought of celebrating my birthday that way before even though my Non Profit, the Now & Later Effect, caters to the homeless. I had been allowing myself to get so wrapped up in celebrating that I forgot to include perhaps the most important aspect of the day, creating something that I would enjoy rather than something that followed what a traditional celebration is. That day was special for more reasons than being blessed with another year. I finally realized that happiness isn't defined by comfort but by purpose! Trying to celebrate in the traditional ways that brought others happiness didn't work for me. I had to step out of the comfort of the norm and what everyone else viewed as a grand celebration and do it on my terms.

I've found that one of the most important pieces in the whole scheme of things is your relationship with God. He's so perfect that he has blessed us to enjoy doing what we are created, purposed to do. Obtaining the spiritual discipline that can transform your mind and desires to reflect God will lead you directly to your happy place. There's something so fulfilling about putting all of your energy and strength into God instead of worrying about getting any thing and in turn, colliding with your desire for Happiness. God loves us and wants to see us prosper. When we trust Him with our desires while focusing on the purpose He put inside of us He handles the light work and leads us to Happiness. He's so good! Trust Him.

He's planned a way for you that will lead you to your best life...
"Happy are those that keep His decrees and seek Him with all their heart" Psalm 119:2

The Search is Over

We've all been there... rummaging around at the bottom of a bag or drawer for that thing we can't seem to find. It's hard to give up and stop looking for it because "We just saw it..." " Just had it a second ago..." or "Know it was right there..." Finally, we give in and figure out an alternative for the moment because we know that continuing to look without finding it, will only add to our frustration or confusion. And then, hours later when you're not looking anymore, it finds you.

I can't tell you how many times I've been confused about major decisions in my life and instead of allowing things to happen organically, I run searching high and low for something to fill the void. I won't say that I haven't had awesome experiences because of this but more often than not I am distracted by things along the way that ultimately threaten to bring my journey to a halt. The reckless abandonment that comes with trusting God allows you to rest in his promises and the things that you know to be true. If you know your happiness is something that you will definitely receive you can focus your attention on something different altogether. Trying to pinpoint where it is, where its coming from, and who or what will bring it will have you thinking everything is Happiness and your skepticism will likely cause you to miss it when it does show up. One of the many things I learned in class at the Studio is that when acting, if something isn't working to help you achieve your goal for the scene, you have to change your approach. At some point in life you will have to decide if you want to keep going in the same circles searching for Happiness as if it's a destination or change the approach and focus on doing things that create an atmosphere for it. When you know that you will receive it you'll be able to find joy even in the difficult moments that may come your way. If you will allow yourself to see past your current situation and keep a tunnel vision on what you know is yours, you won't have to go looking for Happiness because it will find you.

A New Start in Old New York

Dre and I finally made it to New York in March and almost instantly, the tests of faith and perseverance began. Leading up to the big day I still had so many unanswered questions but because I knew the move was a necessary step, I was prepared to take it even with all the risks involved. I'd made up my mind to follow what I felt like God was telling me to do whether it looked good on the surface or not and then I received a call the week before our arrival date that a friend's roommate had just moved out of nowhere and now, the room was open. I was excited, amazed, and felt that it was no doubt, a move of God. She set up a conversation with her friend and owner of the building to speak with me regarding the availability of the room and after speaking with her about a few things (including her concerns about not having window guards in the unit) she said she had to look into a few things but assured me that it would probably be okay to move in. That same week a job I had previously applied for and since realized that maybe the company wasn't interested, reached out to me to "come in and fill out paperwork." What?! I was AMAZED! I felt like everything was coming together and couldn't wait to arrive at my new beginning.

Our flight landed and I watched as Dre became as fascinated with New York as I am. I watched his eyes grow bigger and bigger experiencing Times Square for the first time… All of the different people, cultures, cuisines, etc peaked his imagination and I LOVED IT! But just a few days into our move I was told that because of the window guard laws we wouldn't be able to live at the place I thought I'd secured. I went in to speak with the lady regarding the job and learned that after reading a post on my blog, jamiedreamsbig.com, she knew prior to even interviewing me that I was the perfect person for the position. But I also learned that because of all of the paperwork required it would take 2-3 months to start. We were now without a home, a source of income, and because I didn't have the necessary proof of work, unable to find a home. We moved around a lot! I was back to pulling

50lb bags in and out of subways but this time, I had a stroller, a child, and we can't forget, his bag of toys. I ran into situations that I would've NEVER been able to plan for and had to use every resource available. The people that have always been there for me were and some of the people that I thought would understand and support seemed to only be available to help if it was convenient and there was no risk involved for them. It's been hard and it's been absolutely crazy, but it's also been humbling!

One night shortly after eating at one of the hotels we stayed in I realized I was still hungry. I wondered why and had a moment where I searched my mind for the thing that would satisfy the craving. I soon realized I wasn't hungry for food. It was my purpose, my happiness, that thing inside that nudges you and says "Keep Going! There's more to this!" growling loud enough to catch my attention like an empty stomach in a quiet test room. I realized that all of these things were providing me with the necessary lessons I need to really be able to operate in my ministry to the homeless and to create the life I've always wanted. I realized that these trials and lessons didn't mean that I wasn't doing my part and that no matter how far I got in life, there would always be a lesson or something to be learned. Things still aren't perfect and I feel conflicted with the happiness and peace I feel and what it looks like on the surface because right now, the picture isn't a pretty one. Even as I write this, I am unsure of so many things. But I am sure of God's presence in my life and the purpose that He put inside of me to minister to the less fortunate and push people to live life to the full extent of their capabilities. He is constantly making a way and regardless of the risks, I will always take them. So yes, I may have to go through these tests and trials and I may have to fight through the bad days to get to the best days of my life! But it'll be worth it! I'm stronger and my faith is stronger because of this! I'm smarter because of this! And my relationship with God is on another level! I may feel like I'm failing at times… but as long as I'm failing forward, It's worth it!

How far are you willing to go for happiness? Would you risk being afraid, unsafe, confused, or unhappy? Well that's where I am… The picture of Happiness in my mind isn't about being in New York or even necessarily fulfilling my dreams. It's about doing everything I can to obtain the level of Happiness I know God wants to me to have and feeling his presence on this journey with me even when things aren't perfect. It's about me fulfilling HIS dreams for my life. I know it gets rough sometimes and giving up can seem like it's so much easier. Trust me, I understand! I want to encourage you to stay in the race and to enjoy the scenery along the way. The benefits are worth the risks involved and you are strong enough, intelligent enough, and as long as you remember that happiness isn't a destination, but the entire journey itself- You'll be happy. If you're ready for the journey that happiness is, it's time to put your walking shoes on. And pack light…

"Don't settle for less. Even a genius asks questions…" Tupac

Jamie Berry is a Blogger, Founder and CEO of nonprofit organization the Now & Later Effect, and Inspirational Speaker Jamie Berry has been spreading inspiration with her transparent and upfront speaking and writing style for years. A native of Fort Worth, TX, Jamie has made a life of defying odds and expectations by turning the broken pieces of life into a perfect portrait and works tirelessly to help others do the same.

The Art of Healing

I was born into this world three months early as a preemie and almost died; but I fought to keep living. My entry into life taught me how to become resilient despite any traumatizing circumstances. I was born and raised in a city that has been plagued and labeled as one of the most dangerous and impoverished cities in America. This is a city that put America on wheels, where blacks from the south migrated for a better opportunity. But in return have been neglected by the government and physically poisoned from the lead in the water.

My city taught me to keep reaching and to never settle, because there's always something better out there to feed your soul and spirit. Flint, Michigan aka Fli-City is the place that made me who I am today. I took dance classes in a recreational center that operates right in the heart of the hood. My daily drives to dance class was a combination of feeling depressed, sometimes unsafe but somewhat intrigued by all of the things I witnessed around me.

From constantly having to dodge the deep potholes in the roads, to ignoring all of the boarded up houses, seized businesses and casually laughing at all of the crack heads and prostitutes that strolled up and down the streets in torn up clothing with an absurd strut. My environment became the definition of oppression. This was my world, my home and my reality.

My father had the mission and determination that my siblings and I would not become another statistic, so I trained to work very hard at my dreams. I understood what discipline and focus was as early as 5 years old.

My parents decided that my sister and I

would attend school on the South side of town instead of the North side, where we lived because the schools were too rowdy and the education was poor. So we used my grandma Willa's address and pretended that we lived on the South side.

In the 3rd grade I learned first-hand what bullying was. Boys began to explore their sexuality and would make fun of young girls who breasts were not developing as fast as other girls in the class. I was that little girl that boys would pick on. I guess this was their way of saying they really liked me. But in return it did nothing but destroy my confidence and self-esteem.

I started to pray that my breasts would grow faster. I became so insecure about my body that I started to shop for boy clothes or loose fitting clothes that hid my figure. Maybe they wouldn't notice how awkward I looked, but at the end that strategy didn't work.

In the 4th grade, I still had the same bully. It got so bad that I ended up telling my father about it. I remember him picking me up from school one day and making me point him out. My father went up to the little boy and scared him so much that when I returned back to school, the little boy didn't even make eye contact with me. Unfortunately, that only lasted for a few weeks. He was back to the same behavior shortly after.

By the 5th grade, I was bullied pretty frequently by another male classmate to the point where he would touch me inappropriately. Sometimes he would touch me on my butt or on my inner thigh and I would sit there, frozen from fear. He would hit me and threatened that if I ever told the teacher on him that he would treat me even worse. So I kept quiet.

My only escape from this unhappiness was to go to the office and pretend that I was sick. I would call home all of the time and say that

I didn't feel good, just so that I didn't have to deal with being bullied. This plan started to become my monthly routine, I was always sick. But my parents never really paid close attention to the fact that I was pretending. They never grew suspicious to the idea that maybe something was going on with their child at school.

Every night before I would go to bed, I made a special prayer that I wouldn't get picked on at school the next day. I hated school so much because it wasn't a safe space for me. I never once felt protected.

I didn't believe that my prayers were being answered because the bullying heightened when my teacher assigned me to classroom seats and had me sit right next to guy who bullied me so much. My faith was vanishing and I slowly started to contemplate suicide. I was not happy at all.

It was hard for me to understand how someone could want to cause so much harm to me every day and I had never done anything. I felt so helpless. This made a huge impact on my social life, I didn't trust any of my peers, I became even more introverted and was afraid to speak my opinion because I didn't want to become another target.

Middle school was a little more of a breeze for me. I decided to overcome my fears. My skin had toughened and I didn't let anyone walk over me anymore, not even my bully from elementary school. I confronted him and told him how much his mistreatment effected me. It was through this assertiveness, I had less and less problems with the boys in my class. I remained focused on my schoolwork, socialized less and less and vowed to myself that I wouldn't spend any time and energy on finding a boyfriend or just dating.

High school came around and my main objective was to finish all four years of school with honors. I was solely focused on strengthening my artistic skills so that I move to the east coast and attend art school. I could care less about popularity, being accepted or being understood. Because one thing I grew to realize was that the only person I could depend on for happiness, security and loyalty was myself.

The more that I came into my own skin and understood that this young girl was transitioning into a young woman, the less friends I associated with. I also was being challenged to confront the person that bullied me in elementary school.

At this point in my development my core beliefs were extremely strong. When all of my female friends were already sexually active and dating, I was still a virgin waiting for marriage. I looked at love and sex as something sacred, pure and spiritual. I romanticized about what type of man I would fall in love with once I moved away from home. I dreamed about what my husband would look like, the artistic things he would do, how he would walk and speak.

It was finally time for me to pack my things up and head east where I would be attending The University of the Arts as an Illustration major. When I tell you that I was anxiously ready to go, I was ready. No tears were dropped, just a huge smile across my face and an open spirit and mind.

I was excited about meeting individuals who were on the same level as me, and more. I needed to be challenged and to gain further exposure of the arts and life.

This was one of the greatest times of my life. This was exploration time, growing into being an adult time, make responsible decisions time. I met some really great people who introduced me to new ways of thinking, new spiritual practices and a healthier diet. My only stress was completing my homework deadlines and making sure that the work that I was producing was good enough to pass each class.

Freshman year was a success and it was time for me to go back home for the summer to regroup. Lucky for me I took on some commission jobs that kept me pretty busy. Those jobs were able to pay for my plane ticket to go to California where my sister was invited to teach at a tap festival.

Really great faculty members were scheduled to be there and I did not want to miss the opportunity of learning from such talent. Furthermore, I was excited to be amongst Hollywood stars, some of best of the best in the entertainment industry. But I didn't know that my life would shift drastically. I didn't know that my innocence and fragility would be targeted and taken advantage of by one of the very same people whom I looked up to in the entertainment industry.

August 18, 2003 is a night that I will never ever be able to erase out of my memory.

I was interrupted out of my sleep by a knock on the door at 3:30 in the morning. The only reason why I decided to open up my hotel room door was because of the familiar face that I viewed through the peephole. There was nothing inside of my mind that brought me to understand the reason why he would be knocking on my door in the middle of the night.

I was 18 years of age, a virgin with the youth of a child. I had no sexual experience at that time and he had no right to be in my room. None.

He saw me as his primal target and abused the fact that he was older than me that I respected and looked up to him as a mentor. He abused his "status" and my trust in him and instead replaced his intentions with evil motives.

His spirit intimidated me so much that

chills trickled down my spine and just like that, I froze.

My only survival tactic was to remain still and silent just like I did with all of the other times that I was bullied and touched inappropriately in elementary school. I just sat there in complete shock and terror.

He kept telling me, "You have a very innocent spirit. Do you know that?" The more uncomfortable and stiff I became in his presence, the more he tried to assure me that he was a gentleman.

My soul was robbed and I had no strength to physically stop what was happening to me. Before I knew it, I was being penetrated and my virginity was being stripped away.

Because I didn't physically fight him off, it was harder for me to grasp what I had just experienced. I knew that what happened wasn't right or normal, but I began to feel guilty for not doing more. So I kept quiet and didn't tell anyone until 2-3 weeks later. Silence became my best friend, and it started to eat away at my mind, body and spirit. I fell into a deep, deep depression.

The fact that I physically froze to the point of never fighting him off, I guess made him assume that it was consensual. But it wasn't. Consent would have been him asking for permission to 1. Come to my room. 2. Me telling him "yes" it's okay for you to come to my room at 3:30 in the morning, it's okay to lay in my bed, to kiss me. 3. It's absolutely FINE to invade my space and penetrate me. BUT none of those experiences were granted through consent.

He took advantage of my innocence and that was his power. I remember after the rape was over looking at the blood on the white sheets.

There was blood everywhere. As soon as he left the room, I quickly grabbed the sheets off the bed, crumbled them up, ran down the stairs to another hotel floor and threw the balled up sheets in a corner. I made sure no one was looking and quickly ran back into my room. That was my way of trying to erase what happened to me.

I began to view everyone in my environment as predators. There was this humiliation and embarrassment that continued to haunt me. I had to get out of this misery, so I finally decided to speak out. My sister was the first person that I told and just like that my story and experience was circulated amongst my intermediate family; close friends and tap dance community. It became a nightmare.

They wanted to know the specific details of what happened, why didn't I tell them sooner, etc. My phone rang non-stop. The more they wanted me to share my experience, the more I began to go into a cocoon. I was petrified. I felt humiliated and embarrassed. What was worse was finally trying to report it to the law. The social worker told me that it would be even harder for the justice system to retrieve evidence that I was raped, because it took place in a different state and because I wasn't under the age of 18.

I was also reminded that I would have to relive my story over and over in court. The court would want to know every last detail of what happened and that I should anticipate being interrogated. There was so much information being fed to me all at once and my only concern was my sanity.
Again, just as I was born into this world fighting for my life- I had to revert back to those same survival skills but in a different way to again, fight.

I was fighting for a peace of mind and my personal truth. It was very tough, especially with no one ever coming to my immediate rescue. I was left to fight this battle alone. The only support I received from my family was through words and a card. I felt abandoned.

Instead of taking the time to love and heal myself, I began to depend on love from men. The neediness and dependency on feeling the void of coping and healing the right way was being ignored. This resulted in accepting abuse as normalcy in my relationships. My inner voice was being ignored constantly.

It wasn't until I ended my toxic relationship with men that I began to start healing. This gave me the strength to become courageous and overcome being raped, belittled and bullied.

Slowly but surely, I began to find my voice and the courage to speak out about my experience. First I started to spend a lot of time in my solitude and honored whatever it was I felt that my spirit needed at that moment in time.

I began to write when it was too difficult for me to speak my truth. Instead, I began to share my story in my artwork.

In my early twenties I was still trying to get comfortable in my adulthood and I had a lot of questions about womanhood. I didn't understand every aspect of it nor did I understand all of the pain that I was still feeling from being raped. I wanted answers.Womanhood or Woman's-Hurt? was the first question I began to explore.

This thought led me to create an autobiographical art series and documentary that both expose the ills and truths on how "rape culture" has become an abhorrent norm.

My story and project has now become a part of a international movement and has been the voice for women who have never ever found the courage to speak up about their past trauma.

Through my personal trauma I have been able to find my life's purpose.

So many women throughout the world have been raped. Most often, we are raped between the ages of 16 and 19, at the time when we are transitioning from adolescence to womanhood. This forces us from a state of innocence and inexperience into a whirlwind of hurt and pain as we work through the blame, shame and guilt that is casted upon us when we speak up about our experience. And this is how womanhood becomes woman's hurt.

Rape is an act of warfare against the victim, their family and their community. It is vicious, unrelenting and ravaging.

Rapists negatively affects the full potential a girl can contribute to herself, her family and her community because their actions are highly detrimental to the physical, psychological and emotional state of the victim.

Like a terrorist, the rapist leaves the victim and their families reeling, overcome by fear, anger and anxiety as they work to pick up the pieces.

So the healing process is not just for the victim but for everyone affected by such a tragedy. It forces everyone to be accountable, to make choices and take serious glances into the mirror to stand up to support, protect and fight for the survivor; and to deal with the rapist accordingly. But, when families, bystanders and communities don't stand up and fight, and just sweep rape under the rug, it becomes extremely painful and lonesome for the survivors.

So I fight, despite the lack of protection and respect from some of my family and community members because deep down inside I know I am not alone. I know that this is not just my battle.

I have chosen to change the effects of this horrible experience and instead, transform my inner turmoil into the driving force of a "positive call of action" that let's other women and girls know that they are not alone.

I am here to encourage each and every one of you to speak up and shine your light into that darkness. Take the time to celebrate, rejoice and give thanks that you have survived.

Rape is a predatory behavior. Speaking up also tells the predator, I have a conscious, I know what you did to me and it's not okay. It also can potentially stop rapists from committing the atrocious act on another girl, woman, family or community.

But we can't remain silent. We must become warriors to protect ourselves, and the generations of girls that follow us, so that their initiation into womanhood is not accompanied by woman's-hurt. As a warrior, I chose bravery and resilience over silence and fear and Womanhood or Woman's-Hurt? is my story.

Frances Nielah Bradley is a visual and performing artist from Flint, Michigan. Bradley has been recognized for her visual artwork by the National Conference of Artist in Philadelphia and received the Artist Legacy Award. She was also awarded studio space through 40th Street Artist in Residence (AIR) Program. She is the creator of art series, Womanhood or Woman's-Hurt: The Art of Healing, an autobiographical, visual testimony of surviving sexual assault.

The Case of the Ex

I HATE YOU! I WISH I NEVER MET YOU! YOU'RE A SELFISH ASSHOLE, YOU'RE A DEADBEAT DAD! IM CHANGING HIS LAST NAME TO MINE….. This was the common dialogue me and my son's father had on a regular basis during my pregnancy and within the first year of my son's existence. But we weren't always this way… Once upon a time, it was I LOVE YOU! YOU'RE THE BEST THING THAT EVER HAPPENED TO ME! YOU'RE MY BEST FRIEND! WE WILL BE TOGETHER FOREVER! It was 3 years of love, 2 years of chaos and 2 years of hell. That was 7 total years of allowing someone to have a hold of me mentally and physically. 7 years of not wanting to let go. 7 years of my life…. It's a hard pill to swallow on why it couldn't and didn't work. I know better now but took a long time for me to get to that place of content, forgiveness and moving on. To understand how I got to the point of utopia, you have to understand our beginnings and where we have been. So let me take you back to our honeymoon stage and beginnings.

It all started my junior year 2005 at the university I was attending. I had just crossed into my distinguished sorority and my Line Sister would always tell me that her friend David would always ask about me and want to take me out. Let me tell you about David. He was a handsome and Greek affiliated as well, always dressed nice and was the life of the party. He was a gentleman and always had good conversation. Seems perfect to my 21-year-old self... right?? Well at the time, I had a boyfriend so my response was always "tell him thank you but I got a man". He was never rude or disrespectful with me. When I would see him around campus, small chat and a simple hi would be sufficient enough for us. I always thought he was handsome but loyalty kept me from his advances and taking it beyond friend status. Well a few months later, me and my "man" that I had been with for a year were no more so I was once again a single 21-year-old looking for love and fun. One weekend in September, David's fraternity ended up having a party at their frat house. It was packed with probably 60 college men and women, bottles upon bottles of liquor and Jamie Fox's Unpredictable album blasting through the house so needless to say… we were all feeling pretty good and having a hell of a time. As it got later and the party was dwindling down, I decided it was time to exit. As I was walking out of the house to my car with my Line Sister, a burgundy Buick pulled up to me and to my surprise it was David with a huge grin on his face. We exchanged a few words and he told me to hop in the car with him and let's ride to listen to some music. We did just that. We rode around the city listening to music and that night was the beginning of my long lasting relationship with David.

See, I knew the reputation David carried on campus, a lady's man. I heard the stories and knew some of the hearts he broke, but of course, I knew I was different. We dated for a whole year before we made it official. But that first year prior to us officially being in a relationship, love was felt, scars were beginning to formulate, enemies were created and dangerous habits surfaced. When we first started dating, we hung out tough. He would invite to me his house to hang out with his frat brothers and friends. He would take me with him when he went home and introduced me to his mother. We just were spending lots of quality time together. But alongside those moments, were not so great moments. There were times where I didn't hear from him for days which caused me to become unsure. I started questioning, is he still into me? Is he hanging with another female? What am I doing wrong? But I stuck it out because in my young mind, I knew that if I could convince him that I was the woman he needed, he would eventually cut everyone else off and just be mine. Although we were spending a lot of time together, there were still other women. I knew those periods when I didn't hear from him, he was entertaining another, especially one in particular. She was close to him and his frat and made it a point to be wherever he was. Even though in my eyes, she never compared, but she was my competition. Then came the subtle signs of substance abuse (alcoholism). We all thought it was fun watching him get drunk and want to fight the whole club. I mean, we were in college and that's what most college kids do. But in the back of my mind, I could see there was a fine line between wanting to drink and needing to drink. But in my mind, we were building momentum and I wasn't going to voice my concern because I did not want to get eliminated, so I just kept my mouth shut thinking that too shall pass.

Today, my 32-year-old self couldn't imagine dating someone with those types of behaviors. Being that I started this journey with him at 21 years of age year I only saw the fun, loving, party boy that I wanted to be mine and I would worry about the rest later. That good old saying "We teach people how we want to be treated" played a huge part in how the duration of our relationship played out in that first year. I knew he was messing with other girls. But in my mind, I had the logic "Well… we are not official so who am I to get mad?" I had to swallow my pride and keep in mind that eventually if I continue showing him how much I care and hanging out with him, he will ultimately give me my rightful girlfriend status, so I stuck it out. Looking back at it now, I was tricking myself into thinking that how we were dating was ok. Ladies, if a man wants you, even in the dating phase, he will want you and ONLY you. I knew that wasn't how I was raised nor was it what I was accustomed to seeing in other positive relationships I was around. I remember one night, David and I were supposed to hang out later. He never called or answered my texts. Silence. So I convinced my roommate to drive me to his apartment so that I could spy on him. With his car parked outside and my friend in the car, I entered the building to his apartment and stood outside his apartment door. I didn't knock. I just stood there and put my ear to the door to listen. I listened to the soft music playing inside the apartment. I listened to the moans and quiet screams from a female voice. I was stuck standing there in disbelief and shock. After what seems like eternity standing at the door, I quietly walked back to my friend's car and we drove home. I made up some lie to her when she asked what happened but in my mind, I knew what had happened. And like my 21-year-old self, I never said anything to him because of the excuse "well we aren't together" and I silenced my cries. My world felt like it had ended. I was disappointed because I knew that I deserved more respect than that. Those feelings of… why not me? What does he find in her that he doesn't find in me? I was just an angry, confused 21-year-old that was witnessing the disrespect right in my face and I couldn't and didn't say a word.

David never knew I was outside his door until I confessed to him about 5 years later. I hadn't known then, but later found out, that I was standing outside the door of a life changing moment, not only for him but for me as well… It was at that very moment where David conceived his first born daughter, Harmony. Shortly after David found out he had a baby on the way, he asked me to be his girlfriend. I was happy and honored because I felt like I won. I felt as though I had beat the odds and was the main one, the one he loved, the one he cared about, ultimately beating out the other women. In my mind, I had something to prove to everyone particularly the past women in his life and his child's mother that I was important enough for him to leave all that foolishness behind and be a faithful man. I felt like I had the power because I could change him to be the man I knew he could be. In a way, I stopped caring about him having a child during our dating phase. I felt as though our relationship was more important than that little bump in the road. With Harmony being born, it brought me and

David closer. Our relationship became a distraction to the reality that a baby was coming. We were a unit. If she had something to say to him about them being together or why it didn't work out, he would tell me what she said and in turn, I would feel like I needed to protect him and our relationship by addressing those issues she had with him to her. We carried on with our relationship as if there was no baby. We even moved in together in the months leading up to Harmony's birth. While fighting those battles for him though, I formed an enemy… the angry baby momma. There were times we had exchanged words so intense that I left the girl crying on the phone constantly. I threw it in her face that he's mine and that you're going to have to deal with "us" being around their child.

The next 2 years were fairly happy! We were living together. Most of our mutual friends were friends so it was nice hosting things at our house and being a family. We even got a dog that symbolized something that we took care of together. But slowly, those happy times became less and less and I started to notice different sides to David. As the drinking was starting to noticeably become more of an issue, we were starting to argue more. I would have to stop him from fighting others when we went out due to his drinking and it all just became too much as a young college student. But when he wasn't drinking on the weekends, he took care of me emotionally and physically. He was sweet and a great listener. He worked 2 jobs to make sure I felt provided for. He had good intentions but paranoia mixed with drinking always got the best of him. We would break up to make up and act as though nothing ever happened. Because I was young and immature, I started to develop a temper. Something that I never really had prior to him. I noticed that my words were becoming harsher and my attitude was becoming more ill because I was reacting off his behaviors. This being my first "real" relationship, I never really knew how to handle conflict with a boyfriend, so I always resulted to verbal and physical fights. With the exception of one incident, David never hit me back when I would attempt to be physical with him. He always tried to restrain me and calm me down, but that anger was just piling up that it started to become repetitive and automatic to want to throw something at him or try to hurt him. It's never ok for another human being to be physical with one another. Never! That is something that I regret and feel remorse about to this day. I would never want my son going through something like that and will forever be sorry for my actions towards him. I got too comfortable getting physical with him, throwing things across the room at him to express my frustrations.

Even through all that, he still loved me because he knew that he was causing a lot of burdens and as a result, he still struggled with his personal demons. Looking back, playing house that young, I wasn't mentally and emotionally ready for it. There were always issues with potential cheating and his constant flirting with other women. He was persistent at using social media and other avenues to converse with new women and I constantly found myself arguing with females because of it. It made me insecure. I can recall a time where I was going to travel an hour away to a nearby university just to confront a woman that thought it was ok to call my man at 2 am in the morning. Pure craziness! The nights we would all go out drinking with friends and to the clubs were becoming more of a chore than fun. When David got drunk, I would become public enemy #1 to him. It got so bad some nights, one late night in particular he tormented me by throwing glass plates at me at a restaurant. There were some nights to avoid the arguments and his behavior when he would come home drunk, I would leave to go sleep in my car with my dog in fear of going to a friend's house or my parents' house because I was too embarrassed to tell them the what's, why's and how's. Even though we were in bad spaces, I still felt the need to protect him from outsiders. It's almost as if he was my child, the type of love and protection I wanted to shield him from. I believe in the back of my mind, I knew he could be a good man, he just wasn't living to his fullest capabilities. I never wanted anyone to think of him in a negative light. We tend to protect the ones we love, even if they treat us disrespectfully. However, it wasn't until the plate throwing incident at the restaurant that I knew something had to change because I was turning into an angry spirited person. A year later to escape the madness, I moved to another city where I accepted a position at a dream job. However, after almost 2 years of back and forth, we were back together and he moved to the city where I was living.

Things were good for about 4 months but then slowly but surely, those issues that were never resolved and that haunted us prior were creeping back into our lives. We broke up 5 months of him being there but we still were living together. The next 6 months were madness. Text messages from other women, not holding his weight in terms of finances, the drinking, all of those themes became the daily norm for us. It got to a point where I felt like I needed to leave again because that was the only way to break the cycle. I made the decision to go back home to get a piece of mind while he stayed in the city and continued to work and live his life. During the time I moved back home, David kept trying to get back with me and I kept dismissing him. He would pour his heart out to me and I would just stomp on it like an ant because I was still hurt from all the madness that had occurred with us. At this point, I didn't feel sorry for him. I didn't want to protect him, I wanted to hurt his feelings by any means necessary because of all the hurt and pain he put me through.

I had lost all respect for him and it showed through my verbal communication and lack of caring.

    I thought that in order to get over him, I needed to find someone to replace him. This was hard for me because we had been together for about 6 years and he was the only man I had dated or been with in that time period. I quickly learned that the grass isn't always greener on the other side so as soon as that failed as a result of the guy cheating on me, I ran to my comfort blanket, David. It was just easy for me because I knew him and didn't have to essentially go through the dating phase. He would start to visit me and I went to visit him on multiple occasions like old times. But this last time I went to visit him was different because it was that moment, that we conceived our soon to be son. We were not together but just messing around when I found out I was pregnant. I had mixed emotions because I was nervous but somewhat happy because it was with someone I had known for so long and I thought he would share the same excitement but it was at that point where the tables were turning and it went from chaos to hell and the man I thought I knew was gone forever.

    Physically I had the best pregnancy I could think of. I didn't have morning sickness or gain a lot of weight. I had a glow for days. But mentally and on the inside, I was a mess! The David I had grown to love and knew for so long had disappeared and this new David that I thought I knew hated my guts. The day I told him I was pregnant, he asked was it his? That crushed my world because he knew I wasn't that type of girl. He didn't participate in any doctor appointments and would come into town and not check on me. I would go see him only to get stood up for basketball games and other trivial things. I was willing to clean the slate and start fresh. Anything that happened before hand didn't matter because we were preparing to bring a life into this world. Knowing that I was going to be a mom changed my ways and perspective on things. Things I thought were important, just weren't. The way I would get angry seemed to have been lifted from my shoulders. I was a completely different person and I just so desperately wanted him to see that side of me. He didn't see it as such. If it wasn't for my parents, I don't know what I would have done. They gave me guidance and cared for me as I was creating life. There were times I would literally throw up from crying so hard from begging him to be with me and our baby and he just didn't see that. I even gave him $1000 of money I had saved for the baby because I thought if he wasn't so concerned about getting more money, he would focus on us but that was just a waste of time and energy because things continued to be the same. I finally realized that sometimes you have to lose yourself to find yourself.

Once Jaxon was born, my life changed forever. Things that I thought were important to me just didn't matter anymore. I had someone else looking up to me. Once my son came into this world, and with the continued disrespect from him, my desire to be with his father became more of a distant memory. Through my son, I gained the confidence to know that I deserved better. Each day, as my focus shifted from David to our son Jaxon, I became a stronger minded individual. There was a power that took over me. The feeling and responsibility that I had a person looking up to me and to take care of empowered me for the good. The change didn't happen overnight. There were still issues with other women and that desire to be a family. The true turning point wasn't until I later learned that he thought he impregnated another woman. It wasn't the fact that he possibly got another woman pregnant, it was the fact that he was doing all the things for her during her pregnancy (driving to 3 hours away to go with her to doctor appointments, spending time with her, caring for her) that I desperately wanted him to do for me. It angered me beyond words because I couldn't even get him to pay the $120 a month we agreed upon. All of that anger turned into my "aha" moment and I realized that he isn't the person for me...period.

Reflecting on the day we met and to the point that I knew he wasn't the person for me, I could see so clearly the errors of my ways. David and I should have never been in a relationship... period. We shared similar interests but who we were as individuals should have never been mixed together. Wanting to care for a man and protect a man is great but when it gets to a level of protecting them as if they were your child, it's usually a recipe for disaster. You have to let a man be a man. You can't shield them or protect them on that level. Even if you are the bread winner in the relationship, you can't throw that in a man's face. There are roles we as women hold that we can't reject to take on a man's role. Words last forever so choose them wisely. As I reflect on our relationship, a lot of my anger haunted me down the road like during the time I was pregnant. He hated me for the things I said to him in the past. Not to say it was right and even if he did deserve the things I did and said, I should have taken different avenues to channel my anger. Communication was never right in our relationship. If you can't talk things out or even have the capable to discuss the differences, you will never find peace within that relationship. You have to learn how to communicate with one another in order to build and work through issues. When I became less worried about the things David was doing and became more focused on my son Jaxon and my well being, I started to find my inner peace.

Today, Jaxon's father and I live different lives. I'm in a healthy, loving relationship with a man that genuinely loves me, treats me like a queen and loves my son just the same. It took me some years to actually get back into the dating game because I had to figure out what I wanted, who I was as a woman, mother, and future wife. Ultimately, me cutting off that life support to David was the best thing I could have done for us as co-parents. He quickly learned that the luxuries he once had from me were extinct. The relationship that I defined for us is strictly co-parenting which doesn't include me in his personal business, finances, etc. Unfortunately, the courts help facilitate on the finance end but we decide the time our son spends with each parent. Cutting those ties with David also taught him about ownership and responsibility. Something that's in the forefront of our co-parenting efforts is the fact that he holds the power in how Jaxon sees him. I will never tell him he can't see his son and when he can see his son. He holds that power. It goes back to the point of letting a man be a man. I can't hold his hand and tell him how to do it and when, he has to be responsible enough to lead in building a relationship with his son. You can't let bitterness or ill feelings block a father wanting to be a father to a child. Your focus has to be on the best interests of the child and nothing else. We co-parent the best we can. Every day isn't great and we have our disagreements because there is a level of respect and a mutual love for our child. I tend to not let the bad days have any effect on me. In my mind, Jaxon comes first. No exceptions.

I share my story because I want to show all the lovers out there that have been in similar situations, that there is light at the end of the tunnel. It's all about choosing happiness and knowing when you deserve better. Once you require the respect and love and that's rightfully yours, the sooner others will have no choice but to show you the respect and love you deserve. At the end of the day, you can't make a man want you, he has to want you, desire you and do right by you. No baby, no amount of money will change that. You have to be able to be strong enough to see the signs for what they are and move on to the blessing God has in store for you. I used to ask why God would put me in these situations but I later learned that he was giving and teaching me so much more in regards to life, love and how to be truly happy. Life doesn't always happen as we planned and that's ok. It's all about how we react to trials and tribulations that define our character and makes us stronger individuals. I never thought that I would have a baby out of wedlock or be co-parenting, let alone be treated how I did during my pregnancy by someone that I've known for so long and loved at a one point in time. But as life changes and as women, we learn to adapt. Don't let anyone take or dim your light. I hope through my words, you find the confidence to stay strong, focused and beautiful. Know you are pretty!

Keyaira is a dedicated mother to a vibrant 3-year-old who is the light of her life. Outside of mother duties, Phillips is an 11-year member of Delta Sigma Theta Sorority, Inc. where she uses that platform to provide assistance and support through established programs in her local community. Alongside her community efforts, she enjoys traveling, music festivals, art and doing freelance styling work throughout the Midwest. Keyaira is also working towards the launch of her Children's lifestyle clothing boutique "HarlemsKlubHouse" opening Fall 2016.

The Road to Myself

In September 2015, I began studying at the Terry Knickerbocker Studio. At the start of the school year, my acting coach, Terry Knickerbocker, recommended all of his students go to therapy. I'd never heard an acting teacher give this advice. Initially, it struck me as an unusual request but a very practical suggestion. Sometimes a script will require an actor to access emotional areas that unbeknownst to them can bring up unresolved issues. Terry believes through proper self-analysis we afford ourselves the opportunity to learn this before it becomes a block in delivering honest moments on stage. However, I didn't think therapy would be necessary for me and I had a good reason why.

I was born and raised in St. Louis, Missouri. My parents were beautiful hard-working, Christian folks who were and continue to be well respected in the community. Growing up, my environment was safe and very loving, and my support system was strong and positive. My artistic talents were fostered in school musicals and church choirs. My early public exposure paved the way for a bountiful and successful career that included local theaters in St. Louis, the Broadway stage, and television. From the outside looking in and inside looking out, I had no reason to suffer from any inadequacies of self. Because of that, I believed my insecurities had no significant weight.

Therapy

Despite my logic, the continued encouragement of Terry found me in therapy at the start of the New Year. At this point I figured I had nothing to lose and I felt like I was disappointing him every time I said I hadn't signed up yet. The first month was very awkward. The process of self-discovery through therapeutic practice was new and challenging for me. Initially I resisted because I could not find a logical reason or the need to be on that couch in the first place. I had a great childhood and I'd never been abused in any way, I didn't think I had any significant pain or trauma to talk about!

Therapy and Theology

One month after attending weekly therapy sessions I began to open up. This revelation occurred when I attended a 3-day prayer conference in New York City. It was a powerful conference that focused on the healing power of prayer. Looking back I am so grateful to God for perfectly orchestrating events that led to my healing of past and present pain. On the second day of the conference, I was reminded by one of the speakers that there is no pain, no hurt, and no sin that is too big for God to handle. Knowing that I can cast all of my cares on God and trust that He can and will handle it continues to give me so much peace and joy. I found the very next thing the speaker said to be so illuminating it moved me to tears. She sweetly said, "There is no pain, no hurt, no concern or worry too small that God doesn't care about." He cares about the big and the small. I never considered that the 'little things', left unchecked, have great potential to eventually become the 'big things'. When I heard those words spoken, it was as if I had been granted permission to open up in my therapy sessions in ways I didn't allow myself to before. If all pain and concern - regardless of size - is valid, I told myself I was no longer allowed to judge how small I saw my hurt. I didn't need to experience a 'traumatic enough' event to admit that I was in pain. Once this was settled in me, it didn't take too long for me to open up and give my therapist the opportunity to identify unhealthy patterns in my thinking and decision-making.

My Voice

As a New York City actress, I deal with more rejection than the typical 9-5er. It is the inescapable nature of the business. Before I moved to New York to join The Lion King on Broadway, I had never received much rejection in my career. I began my singing in the church and there is where I attribute my early vocal development. As a child, I was often teased as being my music teacher's favorite because I was always given the good solos in school choir concerts. In high school, I was immediately known as "the girl who can sing" before the upperclassmen bothered to learn my name. Each year I participated in high school musicals I was cast as any given leading role.

Feelings of Defeat

During my teenage years, I began to develop an immense pressure to be the best singer all the time. Somewhere along the way my self-worth was predicated on my quality of singing. I didn't receive any wanted attention from the opposite sex unless I was singing (which also contributed to the pressure). Fast forward to my move to New York City where I was suddenly surrounded by amazing singers who could sing circles around me for breakfast. (Literally, some auditions are so early you may not have time to eat breakfast but it doesn't stop these ladies from wailing their hearts out in the audition room.) As the auditions for other jobs and opportunities continued to be unsuccessful, I began to feel defeated. Accomplished pianist, Kenny Werner, expressed my exact sentiments so beautifully in his book, Effortless Mastery. I began to judge my 'self-worth with every note…enslaved by ego' I was encased in fear. For every audition that went wrong and every part that I didn't receive my self-esteem decreased and impacted my self-worth. This growing insecurity began to spill out in other areas of my life.

A couple of years after moving to New York I met this amazing guy. He was handsome, charming, down-to-earth (which is so refreshing in any major metropolis), and (as he put it) 'financially astute'. I later learned he had money, lots of it. After a couple of dates, I convinced myself that I didn't have enough to offer this man and was not the right woman for him. I envisioned him with an educated, down-to-earth woman who had longer hair, more radiant skin, and a body of a video vixen but the class of a debutante with a notable pedigree, basically what I was unsuccessfully aiming to be. I was certain that any pursuit of this relationship would end in heartbreak and so I left it alone. He didn't chase after me and so I assumed I was right to end it, until I saw on Facebook who he started to date. I admit I judged her. She wasn't unattractive but nevertheless a far cry from the woman I put him with in my mind. In a nutshell, based on pictures she posted online that I scrutinized, this thick, dark-skinned woman was not a debutante. Although my analysis of what he needed in a woman was off, I was satisfied with the fact that this woman and I physically had nothing in common and so my analysis wasn't entirely wrong. Years passed and I found myself looking for him again on Facebook and to my surprise I found that he was engaged – to a Caucasian woman! I do not discriminate against inter-racial love but please understand how this destroyed my analysis! There was no common thread of the women he'd been involved with. That was when I finally had to admit there was something wrong about the terms I created for my happiness, as well as those around me.

It's amazing how our naïve interpretations of painful events as children can dramatically shape our beliefs and ultimately our lives well into adulthood, no matter how far they are from the truth. Not until recently did I realize that I was still carrying the burden of a rejection I had when I was 8 years old.

The Love That Wouldn't Die

At 8 years old, I shared with my closest friends that I had fallen in love! It was actually my first crush. Bobby Matthews was a light-skinned, hazel-eyed boy who lived in my neighborhood. We attended the same church and school. This crush was so intense it lasted for over a decade! I was so convinced that we would be together and eventually get married (I still remember discussing this with his aunt); I was simply waiting on the moment for him to ask me out. Well, as fate would have it, one Sunday out of the clear blue, Bobby walked up to me and quickly and quietly asked me to be his girlfriend. I don't know if it was the excitement of the moment that I had replayed over and over in my daydreams, but I answered, "Huh?" Although he quickly ran away (I did say we were kids), I was so excited. It was the confirmation I was looking for, he liked me and I was about to have my first boyfriend! Now all I needed to do was to get him to ask me that question again so I could answer, "Yes!"

Well that opportunity never presented itself. I gave hints, I gave signs, I asked others to ask him why he hasn't asked again, but he never did. Back then, there was an unspoken rule to allow the boy to initiate any steady interest and that was a rule I was determined to follow even at 8 years old. And so I waited and waited but with great disappointment. For a young girl this was very troubling. All of my friends were starting to date and as I felt left out I blamed myself for the denial of what I wanted most. I constantly thought, 'If only I had just said, 'Yes!' I heard what he said!' I even criticized myself for not running after him after he ran away.Through adolescence, my affections for him only grew but all in vain because Bobby continued to show no sign that he would ask me out again.

Unfortunately, I made it a priority and a challenge to gain his affections. In my mind, I was lacking what was necessary to get him (and for that matter any boy) to like me. I began a search to find out what was wrong with me. Was I too dark-skinned? Did I have too much acne? Was my hair not long enough? Was I too skinny? It was important for me to get to the bottom of this! I knew once I corrected my imperfections I would finally find true love.

When I turned sixteen, life seemed to change overnight. Puberty had finally settled and as my body filled out I began to garner attention from boys that I was not used to receiving. My acne miraculously cleared up and I successfully got permission from my parents to get my ears pierced and trade my glasses in for contacts. I was officially a cool kid. When I returned to high school for my junior year, some of my classmates didn't even recognize me! I relished in the approval. All I could think was I had finally become the woman that Bobby wouldn't be able to resist. To my surprise, everyone else seemed to like me but him. This is when things got ugly.

At the age of 17, I silently came to the conclusion that there was something undetectably wrong with me. I believed I was worthy of happiness but I was feeding myself the lie that I had to earn it. So if I didn't receive praise for my voice or approval for the way I looked, I subconsciously felt unworthy of happiness. I just want to be clear before going on that this ideology couldn't be any further from the truth. This is why I have a fresh excitement when I consider God's grace. I am allowed to be happy because I am His! I am worthy simply because He made me!

The Importance of Self Esteem

So let's address the basics, what is self-esteem? The definition I choose to use is out of Webster's dictionary and it defines self-esteem as a feeling of having respect for yourself and your abilities or a confidence and satisfaction in oneself. Another definition I came across defines self-esteem as having great faith in oneself or one's abilities. One common attribute found in nearly all definitions of self-esteem is the overall opinion of yourself. How do you feel about your abilities and limitations? Do you feel good about yourself and see yourself as deserving the respect of others? How much value do you place on your opinions and your ideas? Do you tend to place more attention on your weaknesses and your flaws or do you focus on your strengths?

Having a healthy dose of self-esteem is important because it affects the overall quality of your life. It greatly influences how well we take care of ourselves and how well we allow others to care of us. It is also important because, as noted before, it is the opinion that you hold of yourself and the only opinion in life you will never be able to escape. Our self-esteem is shaped by our thoughts, relationships, and experiences, including relationships and experiences that stem back all the way from childhood. These are often the main culprits of negative or destructive thinking in us and can have a profound effect on our emotional development through adulthood.

My self-esteem issues began as I continued to seek approval outside of myself. If my peers and critics praised a vocal performance, I felt good about myself. If I received attention from men, I felt good about myself. Nothing is wrong with this either. The problem is if I didn't get sufficient praise or attention, I felt inadequate. There needed to be an overall balance in how much I was being fed from compliments and the lack thereof and that required me to do some inner work and fully recognize my beauty and talents without the admiration of anyone else.

Unfortunately, I kept running into a problem. Feelings are so fickle. The things I felt confident about one day would change the next day. I would celebrate a personal accomplishment in one moment and then reduce its significance in the next. As my abilities changed so would my satisfaction, as the competition of the market changed so would my personal standard of perfection. The way I processed compliments were often influenced by negative thoughts I had entertained moments before. Even as my self-esteem grew I found myself in a depressed way when confronted with failure.

Ronda Rousey

Mixed Martial Arts champion, Ronda Rousey, had an undefeated track record. Her continued success in the ring produced national acclaim and attention worldwide. Her name became popular outside of the ring and brought healthy endorsement deals, numerous film and television appearances, and she became the first woman to cover a UFC 2 video game. Unfortunately her fight to Holly Holm destroyed her undefeated record in less than a minute. In spite of Ronda's undisputed success, after her loss she admitted in an interview with Ellen DeGeneres that she considered suicide. "I was literally sitting there and thinking about killing myself, and that exact second I'm like, I'm nothing, what do I do anymore and no one gives a s-t about me anymore without this", she said. In the very next sentence she states, "To be honest, I looked up and I saw my man Travis was standing up there and I looked up at him and I was like, I need to have his babies. I need to stay alive." The moment she separated her accomplishments and failures from how she defined herself as a woman, a partner, and eventually a mother, she was able to recognize there is great value and worth in her existence.

The Power of Self-Worth

Although I believe a healthy amount of

self-esteem and self-worth is necessary in order to have a quality life, I am biased toward the latter and here's why. Achieving high self-esteem requires me to focus on self, while achieving a great sense of self-worth requires me to focus on my Creator. Self-esteem is based on my external and self-worth is based on my internal. Self-esteem is about what I do and self-worth is about who I am. Self-worth tells me I am not my abilities or lack of, I am great in spite of my mood and the way I feel about myself. I am not what people say or think about me, I am bigger than my experiences no matter how traumatic, and I can't be reduced to my marital status, sex, gender, age, race, political affiliation, class, or any other box society deems to put me in. I am greater than it all!

The journey to building my self-worth began with five steps. These steps required me to get acquainted with my authentic self, become fully aware of my strengths and weaknesses, accept and embrace them through self-compassion and forgiveness, recognize the authority I have in creating my outlook of myself and the world around me, and to give back through acts of service. As I expound on each step, check-in with yourself and take notes on anything that may come to your mind that you may identify with as you read.

My Five Steps to Self

1. AUTHENTICITY

Authenticity is about being genuine. Sometimes we can get so lost in playing a role in order to gain acceptance that we become unfamiliar to who we are in the dark. So, who are you in the dark? What I mean by that is, who are you when you are alone and no one is watching? Who are you when you are free from the fear of judgment? Who are you without any of the roles and responsibilities you or others have given you? What makes you laugh? What are your dreams? What did you want to be when you were a kid? These are all questions I had to ask myself. It may help to sit in a quiet place and imagine a you that doesn't hold the title of wife, mom, daughter, sister, aunt, boss, employee, etc. Imagine stripping off layers that you have collected through life that have covered your true inner self. The core of what you find is the authentic you. This step was the beginning of the road to curing my low self-esteem because it put me in touch with my truth.

2. **AWARENESS**

My second step required me to become self-aware. In order to be aware I must be conscious. Awareness requires you to take a close look at all of who you are, the good, the bad, and the ugly. I had to become curious about my strengths and weaknesses. I allowed myself to find interest in attributes I like and dislike about myself. I became intrigued with destructive, and even constructive, behavior I display towards others and myself. The benefit in becoming aware is identifying areas in your life that do and don't serve you. It allows you to identify a beginning place to develop a nurturing relationship with yourself. Sometimes we choose to be blind to things in us that we don't like because it creates so much pain in us which is why this step almost goes hand in hand with the next step.

3. **SELF-ACCEPTANCE**

This is the step I struggled with the most. Whenever I would hear therapists discuss self-acceptance, I assumed they meant I must submit to the authority of the weaknesses I find in myself. That seemed like a horrible idea to me. Here I am trying to fix the things that are wrong with me and the advice that I'm being given is to just sit back and accept that I'm a mess! (Hopefully you can already detect the error in my thinking. If not, accept that you can't.)

Not until I surrendered the need to be right and perfectly put together did I become acquainted with the powerful, personable, and beautiful me. I chose to become best friends with every part of myself with lots of compassion and even more forgiveness. The key to self-acceptance is loving all of the self you become aware of long enough to get to know who that is before you try to change it and make improvements. A good way to know you are accepting yourself is when self-judgment stops. I refrained from rejecting myself by embracing all that I found in me.

At times it was more challenging to fully embrace my beauty and strengths especially because I have a habit of self-deprecating. When I noticed I was shying away from my light, I reminded myself of the beautiful poem written by Marianne Williamson, "Our deepest fear is not that we are inadequate. Our deepest fear is that we are powerful beyond measure." A good prayer would be to ask God for the courage to accept the good and the bad that you find in yourself. One of the key benefits in accepting who you are is the freedom you gain by seeing your weaknesses as opportunities and not as obstacles. Remember, not until you accept yourself, can others accept you and you accept others.

4. **AUTHORITY**

The two most important authors in my life are the Creator and myself. I had to take a personal inventory. I asked myself who else I had given authority to in my life? Have you given your authority away or have you embraced it? The first authority I needed to RECOGNIZE in the search of myself was that of my Creator. What does God say and think of me? All of the answers I need are in Him because He knew me before I was born and has loved me since the beginning of time. Take time to read Psalm 139. It is my favorite Psalm. God knows our purpose because He created it. As you learn more about your creator you learn more about his creations, including you. Your purpose is generally found in your strengths but can sometimes be found in an area you may deem to be weak. If you feel a calling in an area where you feel inadequate or fearful, find courage in the knowledge that in our weakness, God's strength is made perfect. When we can't rely on our own strength it is the best time for God to show us his power.

The second authoritative power in my life is in me. I am striving to live more and more conscious of the authority I have in creating the life I want by what I think and what I say. So much can be written on this but in a nutshell your whole life has been constructed by the faith you put in the thoughts you house in your head and the words you speak, good and bad.
I recently read the book, Think and Grow Rich, by Napolean Hill. This book has changed my life. I have become extremely sensitive to my habitual way of thinking and speaking. I encourage you to read that book. In it you understand the incredible power behind your conscious and subconscious thoughts as well as ways in which you can shape your life through the power of daily mantras and autosuggestion. Remember, owning the responsibility you hold in creating your life is what gives you authority.

5. ACTS OF SERVICE
Give and it shall be given unto you. What goes around comes around. You reap what you sow. There are so many reminders of this law in life. It's thought provoking to me the science of giving. Giving increases your value. Although I shouldn't give with the objection of seeking praise or validation, when I bless others I feel good about myself. I set in motion the laws and principles that govern this world to receive a blessing. So ironically, building self-worth is achieved by turning our attention away from ourselves and giving back in spite of how inadequate we may feel. I understand that when I serve others I open the door for tangible and intangible blessings.

The road to building my self-worth and self-esteem is a daily choice. It's a daily choice to not compare myself to others and believe that I am enough. I have to make a decision to consciously think positively and weed out the negative. One of the ways I do this is by following the advice of my father. He constantly reminds me and my siblings to surround ourselves with "good books and good people". People and books greatly influence what we think and how we see ourselves. As I make the effort to reconstruct my thinking and surround myself with people who live holistic lives and speak positivity and power, I feel more empowered to value all of me every day.

Currently a resident of Brooklyn, NY, Sophia Nicole's talent has garnered much attention on the New York scene. As go-to singer for The Roots she often provides supporting vocals on The Late Night Show with Jimmy Fallon. She has sung background vocals for Jason Derulo, John Legend, Jennifer Hudson, Charlie Wilson, Sting, Michael McDonald, Bilal, Sara Bareilles, Jasmine Sullivan, Imagine Dragons and most recently featured on the 2nd album promo tour of up and coming star, Gary Clark Jr.

Overcoming Challenges

I grew up in the church. I was a choir member, choir director, usher board vice president, drill team member, youth leader and the church secretary. I was the girl people looked up to and asked to pray with them when they needed prayer. I knew by the age of 12 that GOD had a great calling on my life. I thought because I had a calling, was so active in church, read my bible daily, prayed consistently, praised and worshipped GOD, and was "Saved" that I could never fall short into a sinful life that I had once seen others struggle with. I knew that anybody can fall short of the glory of GOD….I just didn't think it could be me.

January 2001

My good friend and neighbor Michelle and I had stopped into a local grocery Randall's to buy food. While in there I remember it was my step-mother's birthday that day and I wanted to get her a card. I didn't have enough money to buy the groceries and the card so, without a second thought, I decided to slip the card under my shirt and into my pants. I did this all the time and it was no big deal.

As we were grocery shopping, I got an urge to put the card back. I pondered on the urge for a minute and just ignored it. We continued shopping and headed to the check-out line. I was in line and I noticed a cute young Caucasian man kneeling down to look at the magazine on the other side of the check-out line. I waited to speak until it was my turn to pay for my groceries. As the woman in front of me is leaving the check-out, the man makes eye contact with me and I told him I thought he was sexy. He smiles as he begins approaching me and I thought for sure he was going to ask for my number. When he gets within two-feet of me he says, "I saw you put the card in your shirt, you have to come with me upstairs to arrest you." I couldn't believe it; here I was being flirtatious and he was busting me for stealing the birthday card.

I reluctantly gave my car keys to Michelle so she could get back home and pick me up from jail tomorrow morning. It was Sunday night and I knew it would be an overnighter. He took me to a room upstairs in the store and called the police. I tried everything I could to get out of the petty crime to keep from going to jail. When the police got there, they handcuffed me, and took me into Webster County Jail. They took my mugshot, and took me to my cell, where I stayed until the next morning. I should have known that going to jail for the first time, on the first Sunday of the new year, would be an indication of a bad start in 2001. I couldn't believe that I actually went to jail for stealing a birthday card for my step-mother. Who goes to jail over a $2.99 birthday card? Not even a whole three dollars. Apparently, I do. The next morning in court, the judge charged me with 5th degree theft, gave me a fine of $93 which needed to be paid in 60 days and released me. I called my girl Michelle and she picked me up.

A couple of weeks later on 1-21-2001, I went out with my bestie since 6th grade, Audrey and her boyfriend's sister Jamesha. They picked me up at my place, we went to a party and got totally wasted. When the party was over I was headed to the car and I could hear that Audrey and her boyfriend were arguing. They were cussing each other out over an incident that took place in party. Jamesha and I finally got them to calm down. We got in the car and left the party. Audrey was driving like she was in a Nascar race. I remember praying to God to make it home in one piece. We pulled up to Jamesha's place and she got out of the car. I then, get out of the back seat to get in the front. As I sat down in the front seat, I don't even have the door closed and

Audrey speeds off. As we are headed south on 15th street, I closed the door. Something in that moment told me to put on my seat belt as well. As I fumbled to pull the strap over my shoulder, I noticed the traffic light ahead had turned red. Audrey was not slowing down to indicate we were actually stopping for the traffic light. I also noticed head lights headed on the perpendicular street heading east. Audrey sees the car and she speeds up. As she does, I happened to click my seat…BOOM!! "Oh My God! We got hit!" I screamed. The sound of the car colliding sounded like a cannon ball went off in the car. We are spinning around and my body jolted to the left. I feel like we were in a game of extreme bumper cars. As my body jerks back to the right, I hit my head on the dashboard. We continue to spin in a full 180-dgrees now facing north on the other side of the street. As we come to a stop I can feel the entire impact of the accident was on the right side of my body and my head. I remember Audrey asking me, "Danessa are you ok? Let's get out the car." I told her, "I can't move" She was said, "What you mean you can't move" "Like I said, I can't move". She was coaching me on what to tell the police when they got there. "Tell them the light was green".

At that moment, there were some people who came to the scene of the accident, one of them was a male friend from High School. He said he called 911. A few minutes later I heard Corrine's voice, one of my younger sister. "Danessa is that you? Are you Ok?" Even though I knew she was scared, I was so glad that my sister was there. It gave me a sense of relief.

Once the ambulance arrived they pull me out of the car and onto the stretcher. That was the most excruciating pain that I have ever experienced. They got me in the ambulance and put the oxygen mask on my face. Tears began to flow from my face. Even though I was in a great deal of pain, the tears were of joy and thankfulness to

GOD for allowing me to have sense enough in my drunken state, to put on my seat belt. In that moment, I knew that if I did not put on my seat belt, I would have been dead.

When I got to the Emergency Room, they ran tests, X-Rays and CT scans. I was back in the E.R. room when my father arrived. I was glad to see him but I also felt embarrassed. Just a couple of weeks prior, I had been in jail, now a car accident. I felt like I was a disappointment to him. Nevertheless, I think he was happy that I was alive and well.

As we were awaiting the doctor on my results, my father told me that the car accident I was in, was just like the one that killed his 18-year-old sister many years ago. I always knew my aunt died in a car accident because my father had given me her name as my middle name in honor of her. However, I did not know the details of the car accident. I find it ironic that I get into a similar car accident that killed her but kept me alive. I knew it was because God had more for me.

Finally, the E.R. doctor came with the results. For the most part everything was fine, I had some lacerations, bruising and whip lash. However, I did have a multiple hair-line fracture in my right hip. They weren't big enough that I needed to have surgery. The only treatment was pain medication and a set of crutches. They told me it would take 6-8 weeks to heal and sent me home.

By the time I got home, I was in so much pain it took me 2 hours to get upstairs. For the next few days, I went from my bedroom to the bathroom all day long. Often times, Michelle was there to help me out as she watched me cry from the agonizing pain. She got so tired of me crying and complaining that she found 2 random young men to come carry from upstairs and into the passenger seat of my car. Then she drove me to the hospital where I was admitted and stayed for three days.

March 2001

I was recovering well from the car accident. However, I was disappointed that I had to drop-out of college due to absences from the injuries and hospitalization of the car accident. There were a lot of changes taking place in my life and my 3 bed-room town house. Samantha, a friend, and her two children needed a place to stay temporarily and they had moved in. Also my guy John who I had been casually involved with for over 6 months was now living with me as well. John always looked out for me. The first time we hooked up he gave me a quarter pound of weed. That blew my mind. I would get the hook up on marijuana all the time, but that was the first time I got free marijuana. Prior to him moving in with me, we lived 100 miles apart. So when he wanted to see me he sent the money and put me in nice hotels suites. If my car needed repair, he fixed it and paid for it. When I was in the hospital he came to visit me. John was my ride or die. So when he told me that he had a warrant and was on the run and needed a place to hide out, I was down for him. He was always good to me and I knew he cared a great deal for me.

Samantha, John and I were headed to Des Moines to take care of some business. In route my car kept acting funny and was over-heating. We were on 1-35 and pulled into the weight station just south of Ames. We all had warrants and we were plotting on whose name we would use to keep from going to jail. We came up with our false identities. We get out of the car and go into the weight station to use the phone to call for someone to pick us up.

As we explain what is going on the officer says, Danessa are you aware that you have a warrant in Fort Dodge? I was totally taken aback. What? First of all, how does he know my name? Then I realized the only way he could have known my name is because he ran my license plates when we first pulled in. Then I thought why did I have a warrant? Then it hit me, I had missed my court date and forgot to finish paying off the $93 fine. At that moment I thought about using my sister's name but I knew he could match my face with the picture he had pulled up on his computer. So he proceeded to tell me that he had contacted the police in Fort Dodge and they are in route to pick me up. The police arrived and took me back to Fort Dodge. On March 22, 2001 I went to jail for contempt of court. I spent the night in jail and got out the next day.

It was Tuesday, March 27, 2001. Five days had passed since my stint in jail and I was ready to get back on my hustle. I had finished paying off the rest of my fine. I was glad that was behind me. Samantha came to my room to learn how to make a dime and a twenty sack. I had the scale and showed her how much weight for each one. She wrapped them individually and put them in the bag with the rest of the ounce and took the bag back to her room. I tucked my scale away in the closet.

Later that afternoon John wanted to go play basketball. Samantha was going to take the kids to play at the park. They asked me if I wanted to go, but I declined because I was unusually tired. So I opted to stay home and take a nap. I was sleeping good, when I heard a loud pounding on the door. I thought who the hell is knocking on the door like the dang police. The only movement I made was to turn on my side, because I was not about to get out of the bed to answer the door for anybody. As I shifted to a more comfortable position, the next thing I seen when I opened my eyes was a Glock 22 in my face. Immediately, I thought they are here for John. He had been on the news regarding an outstanding warrant. I thought someone had recognized him and told the police he was here. However, the officer with the gun in my face stated, "Danessa we have a warrant to search your premises for marijuana" What the hell? Why was I being raided? Who snitched? I was totally confused. My reply was, "Let me see the warrant".

I get out of the bed and they take me down stair to my kitchen while they are searching. They showed me the warrant. I read it and sure enough it had my name on it. I knew at that point to keep my mouth shut and say nothing else. I knew the only marijuana that was in the house was the couple of ounces that did not belong to me. I didn't know exactly where it was. However, it didn't matter because they found it along with the scale that I had hidden in my closet. I was just glad that we had moved the money the night before.

They read me my Miranda rights, hand-cuffed me, took me outside and into the cop car. I see the entire block is filled with people watching me go to jail. Michelle is watching along with John, Samantha and my younger sister Janet. I was so embarrassed. I was going to jail again for the 3rd time and twice in one week. This time I would be there longer than an over-night visit.

The next day, I had court in the morning. They came to get me out of the cell. When I get in the room, I immediately recognize the judge. It is the same judge that I had just seen six days ago. He remembered me as well. This time he wanted bond money for me to get out. There was no getting out right away. I was being charged with possession of marijuana, possession of marijuana with intent to deliver, possession of drug paraphernalia, and failure to pay a drug stamp tax. I was looking at a few misdemeanors and a class C felony. I then needed a lawyer but I was not working and didn't have any money so I was assigned a public defender. We met and he told me that I had to complete drug counseling in conjunction with my probation. He stated that he was working on getting me out on my own recognizance. I knew that would be a challenge due to my history.

I stayed in jail until Friday afternoon. It was then that I got out and had to go straight to the correctional facility where I would be assigned to my probation officer. I walked into a room where there was about 20 other people going through the same process. They gave us specific instructions on how we were to live life while on probation. I could not leave the town of Fort Dodge unless I got permission from the State. I would randomly be asked to take urine analysis to check for drugs. If they came back dirty, it was a violation and I would go to jail.

April 2001

Once I got home Friday afternoon, I noticed the eviction notice on my door. I had 3 days to leave. I had been gone three days so I really had to be out immediately. Samantha found a small efficiency apartment. It had a small living room, kitchen and bathroom. Samantha, her 2 children, her boyfriend, John and I all moved into an efficiency apartment. It was so small that It felt like we were shoes stuffed into a shoebox. It was not ideal however it was temporary. We moved some of my living room furniture in there because that is all that would fit.

The situation was very stressful. We were into the month of April and John realized that I had not had my period in the month of March. I told him it was late due to stress. In the last 3 weeks, I had been to jail twice, raided and evicted. I probably wasn't going to get it for another week or so. I didn't really pay that much attention but he noticed how I became really irritable and argumentative. I told him that I wasn't happy about how I am living. He continued to insist that it was because I was pregnant.

The next day I scheduled an appointment to go to Planned Parenthood to take a pregnancy test. I went early in the morning alone. I waited in the waiting room pondering the what if? I didn't really plan to become a mother. I had so much experience in helping raising my younger siblings that I didn't want any children of my own. I was deep into my thoughts when they called my name. I got up and they asked me question after question. Then they gave me a cup to urinate in. I went to the bathroom and set the cup in a cubby hole in the wall as instructed. I washed my hands and went back into my exam room.

As I am waiting, a woman came back into the room and told me the pregnancy test was indeed positive. I couldn't believe it. What is the world, was I going to do with a baby? Especially while I have an open drug case and the possibility of going to jail or prison if I messed up again. I was just stuck in disbelief for a few minutes. After the appointment was over, I got into the car and went back to the efficiency apartment. I sat in the car for about twenty minutes to process my entire life. I was scared, nervous, and had no clue how I was going to raise a child.

I went into the apartment. Samantha and John both looked at me and told me, we told you. It was like they knew and only needed the confirmation to prove they were right in the beginning. They both hugged me in excitement. I was not as excited as they were. In fact, I was scared and nervous. I had no job, no car, barely a place to live, had an open drug case, on probation and I was pregnant. Life was definitely not peaches and cream.

May 2001

Waking up on Mother's Day, I thought wow I am actually going to be a mother this year. Samantha and her children left out to go celebrate Mother's Day with her mother. Her family was having a BBQ. She had invited John and I but we wanted to have the small efficiency to ourselves for a moment. We were just glad to have space to walk around without stepping over someone.

This Mother's Day was different because I was finally accepting the fact that I was becoming a mother whether I liked it or not. I didn't have a phone at the time so I would use my next door neighbor's phone to call my own mother in Gary, Indiana to wish her a Happy Mother's Day. It was then that I told her that I was pregnant. I could tell that she only sounded excited because I half-way was. I knew she was concerned because of the trouble that I was in. I told her that I wanted to move to Gary to be closer to her and that I would transfer my probation there. This was a time in my life that I really wanted to be close to my mother, so she could help me with the baby. I had no idea how that was going to happen but I was willing to make it work one way or another.

When I got home, John was smoking a blunt and I knew he would be in a talkative mood. So I began talking to him about our plans for life and our baby. After our conversation, I was in a playful mood, so I started a small pillow fight. We went back and forth hitting each other with pillows. Then he took it to another level and poured a Pepsi over my head. I thought, "wow that is bogus". He ran out of the apartment in laughter. So I go to the kitchen and filled up 2-quart pitcher half-way with water. I went to the door and waited patiently for him to come up to the door. It was quiet and I could hear his foot-steps. When he got close enough I dashed him with the water. I thought it was the funniest thing to see him soaking wet. However, he didn't think so and became enraged with anger. He then knocked me down to the floor and grabbed my hand and dragged me from the entrance of the apartment to the kitchen. I felt like I was in the scene as Tina Turner in the movie, "What's Love Got to do With It". The scene where Ike drags her to the studio. I was trying my hardest to get away but I didn't have the strength. Once he got me to the kitchen. He turned the water on and proceeded to fill up the 2-quart pitcher and dumped it right on my face. He repeated this more than a few times. I literally felt like I was drowning. I was screaming stop, crying and was gasping for air. He continued to do this for what seemed like a few minutes. Once he quit he immediately left the apartment. He left me on the floor crying and scared for my life.

Once I got myself together, I took a bath and walked to Samantha's mother's house. It was about 2-3 mile walk. I remember thinking, how was I going to be in a relationship with a man that would harm me and dang near drown me on Mother's Day, all while pregnant with his child? Life for me kept getting darker and darker. I was crying and walking and I just began to pray to GOD to help me in my situation. I began to repent of all my sins and asked GOD to help me out of this situation with this man. I knew in that moment there would be some lonely days ahead of me if God was going to answer my prayers. Once I got to Samantha's mother's house, I calmed down. I told her what had happened. I enjoyed some food and the moment of being with her family.

When I got back to the apartment, John had been drinking and was apologizing for the episode that took place earlier in the day. He was trying to hug and cuddle. I was not in that mood anymore. He got mad and went to sleep. I didn't care. I just laid there thinking about the day's events. Silently crying and praying myself to sleep. The next day, Samantha's sister stopped by the apartment to say good-bye to Samantha. John was still mad at me and wanted to leave. He asked Samantha's sister if he could catch a ride back to Des Moines. She told him yes and he left with her. He left me and his unborn child in an efficiency apartment. I was a little upset that he would do me like that, but then I thought well

GOD you are working.

July 2001

A couple months later, life was starting to get more stabilizing for me. I had moved in with my father to get back on my feet. I had gotten another job after about a 9-month hiatus of not working. I was attending my court hearings and depositions like I was supposed to. I was seeing my drug counselor and probation officer on a regular basis. I had reconnected with GOD and was attending church regularly. The only thing I needed to work on was getting my driver's license back, getting my car fixed and finding my own place.

I had a couple of visits with my OBGYN and was having a healthy baby. I was grateful and finally embracing the fact that I was becoming a mother of another human being. The time was near that I was having my first ultra sound. As a first time mother, this is the moment that you can actually see the precious human life growing, and developing inside you. This is the moment that most mothers are so excited about. I was so excited that I hardly slept the night before.

Poetry Break

10 O'clock am. The date was 7-09-01.
The day for me had just begun.
It was the day of my first ultrasound.
All that water I drank seems I gained 5lbs.

My emotions were on cloud nine.
Even with all those papers to sign.
In the ultrasound room is where I was placed.
To see your spine, legs, arms and even your face.

It was about 11:15 am when they started.
I got this gassy feeling and almost farted.
I lifted my shirt to expose my big belly.
Next thing I feel is this thick warm jelly.

Soon as I looked at the computer screen.
I couldn't believe my eyes. What a beautiful scene.
Your head down, legs crossed and butt in the air.
Never once showed your privacy and I thought no fair.

I went home with pictures to show and share.
My Dad was behind the front door trying to give me a scare.
I felt so good, happy and very glad.
To show off my pictures of you to your grandad.

I was in the greatest mood
When I received the horrific news
I picked up the ringing phone
To hear a sad tone.

Danessa your mother has just died
For the rest of the day, like a baby I cried.
How could this be, why today?
There was so much I had to say.

Just when there is a lot of good news.
My mother just dies right out the blue.
Plus, in 2days is my baby sister's 17th Birthday.
And GOD decides to take my mother away.

Even though my mother had to depart
I'm still very sad in my heart.
I know everything happens for a reason.
Sometimes people go because it's their season.

The only thing that gives me strength from day to day
Is to kneel down on my knees and pray.
I know I'll never see her precious face again.
Until I reach those golden gates of heaven.

I may not see her beautiful flawless chocolate skin.
But I do have a precious seed within.
If my child is a girl
I will cherish her like a pearl.

I will name her Pameliyah Aalynn
Similar to her grandmother's name Pamela Lynn.
If I have a boy.
I'll still have as much joy.
For I know my Mother's Love
Will be raining from Above.

R.I.P Mom

    I had to notify my probation officer and get permission from the state to attend my mother's funeral because it was in Gary, Indiana. We also had to ride the Grey Hound because I didn't have a driver's license or a car to get there. Money was scarce, so my dad, his girl-friend, and our church family had helped buy the bus tickets for my 2 sisters, my nephew and myself.

    I later found out that she had died of cardiac arrest. I thought that was very unusual since she was only 44 at the time of her death. I thought that was way too young to die like that. However, I knew that her addictions to prescription pill and alcohol could have very well played a part in her death. My mother was often sad and depressed. Most of the time that I had seen her or talked to her she was under the influence of pills or alcohol or sometimes both. A part of me thinks that she wanted to die a long time before then and that she willed herself to die.
I remember seeing her in the casket for the first time. She looked absolutely beautiful and peaceful. She had a slight smile on her face. I knew then that she was right where she wanted to be… in another place.

    The next few months were difficult as I was grieving my mother's death. However, my life was starting to look up. I was starting to see the favor of God on my life. I was accomplishing goals and taking care of business. I had gotten my driver's license back. I had successfully completed my drug counseling program. I had applied for Section-8 Housing and got approved, which never happens when you have an open drug case. But GOD said different.

October 2001

In October, I had my court hearing. My lawyer told me he was going to petition the judge for me to have a deferred judgment. He also told me that he never had a case where the judge actually approved it either. So I was a little discouraged when he told me that. However, I didn't let that deter my belief in knowing what GOD can do in my situation. He told the judge some of the reasons why he believed that I would be worthy of getting the deferred judgment. He explained how I had gotten a job, had clean urine analysis, completed the drug counseling, and had been to every scheduled appointment with him. The judge told us to take a 60-minute recess so he could review the case. About an hour later that judge had made his decision. He approved the deferred judgment. However, he informed me if I missed an appointment with my P.O., went to jail for any reason, or did not pay off my restitution fines that I would be back in court and I would be convicted of all charges and could face up to 10 years in prison. I was to remain on probation for the next two years. If I successfully completed the next two years, then all charges would be dismissed and wiped clean from my record. I was so elated!! I hugged my lawyer and told him thank you. I think he was shocked that the judge actually approved the deferred judgment.

A few days later, I got a phone call from the insurance company regarding the car accident. Apparently, they have been trying to contact me to settle. They offered me $7500 and I took it. I was so excited because now I could get my car fixed, get a place and furnish it. The next week they sent paper work for me to sign and a check in the mail. The first thing I did with my check was pay my tithes in church. I made sure to give back to my church because they had given so much to me.

I had found a nice 2 bed-room house. I moved in at the beginning of November. I had bought a brand new nice Italian leather living set from a friend. My grandmother bought me a bedroom set as an early Christmas gift. I got my car fixed. I had everything I needed by the end of November.

December 2001

On Saturday night of December 1, 2001, I was at my father's house writing a letter to John who had got caught by police and was in jail. When I was done writing the letter I started having contractions. It was about 11:00pm and my sister took me to the hospital. The nurse checked my contractions and admitted me because I was indeed in labor. Two of my sisters, Corrine and Janet, stayed with me all during the process. My male best-friend Jameel, who I had asked to be my baby's God father, got off work around midnight and came to show support while I was in the hospital as well.

I was having complications during my labor. Every time I laid on my left side the baby's heart rate would drop. I had to stay on my back for the rest of labor. Finally, around 8:30 the next morning it was time to have my baby. I still did not know what I was having so I was excited to see what GOD blessed me with. My sisters helped me during my delivery. They encouraged me and held my legs. I was having a difficult time pushing so they used the vacuum to help suck the baby down. Finally, my baby was born at 9:11 am. It's a girl! The doctor yelled. I was so tired. I was glad to know she was here and alive. They laid her on my chest briefly and I immediately welcomed and named my princess Pameliyah Aalynn Singleton. They took her to get her weighed and measured. The doctor was finishing up with the afterbirth. I noticed he was pulling to get it loose from my uterus.

Later that day, my sister Corrine came back to visit me. I had taken a nap with my baby in my arms. When my sister came into the room she came and got my baby. I then got up to go to the bathroom. When I sat down on the toilet, I noticed that there was a lot of blood. I thought, no one told me that you would bleed like you had diarrhea. I stood up briefly and blood was gushing out of me. I decided to pull the call light and sat back down on the toilet. As I waited for the nurse I could tell blood was filling up the toilet.

As I stood up again, the nurse had made it to my room. I stepped away from the toilet and she seen how the blood was continuously gushing non-stop out of me. She replied oh my God you are hemorrhaging. She walked me back to my bed. Blood is everywhere. She called for more nurses and for my doctor to get to the hospital. They have to check my uterus. The epidural has long worn off. So I am in so much pain with them checking me and trying to stop the bleeding. Another nurse was attempting to put an IV back in my hand. She did not know what she was doing because it took several attempt. Another nurse had to step-in and get it done.

I was losing so much blood that I was becoming dizzy and losing consciousness. My doctor finally came and told me that they would have to do an emergency D &C, a Dilation and Curettage procedure. I had to sign some papers to authorize them to do a blood transfusion. As they were transporting me to the operating room, I remember crying and praying. I thought I was going to die. I remember telling GOD that I was not finished with life. I didn't have a baby to leave her motherless like I was now. I remember begging him to let me stay here with her. The next thing I knew they had injected me with pain medication and anesthesia to put me under to do the surgery. When I woke up I was freezing cold. My doctor had

informed me the reason I had hemorrhaged was because part of the placenta was still on my uterus. I was just grateful to be alive. I had to wait for about an hour or so before they took me back to my room upstairs. I noticed the time and was worried that I had missed my daughter's feeding. I was breast feeding and I knew they had to feed her regular formula while I was in surgery.
On my way back up to my room. I was reflecting on the year that I had. I had been through so much and I was just grateful that I made it through the most challenging year of my life. The birth of my daughter made it all worth it. I simply thanked God.

April 2016

There will come a time in your life when all hell breaks loose and you wonder if there is even purpose for you on Earth in this lifetime. However, the many trials and tribulations in that year changed my life forever. In these great lessons as well as the abundant blessings, I learned that sometimes the biggest storms come to attempt to blow you down, drown you out, rain on your parade and even to destroy your life, but in the end they build the survivor to be stronger than the storm itself.

As I reflect back on 2001, I am first grateful to GOD for getting me through it. Even though I do not desire to have a repeat year like this, I am thankful for every jail encounter, the car accident, the raid, the abusive relationship, and even getting through my mother's death. I am grateful because as challenging as that year was for me, it was the start of a foundation of building blocks to who I am today. Sometimes you have to be lost in order to be found. I was definitely a young woman lost in the turmoil of life. I got swept away in pursuing the wrong things in life. What I was doing is not what I knew GOD had for my life. Even though some events I had no control over, I do take full accountability for the decisions that I made in the ones that I did. Galatians 6:7 "Be not deceived; God is not mocked: for Whatsoever a man soweth, that shall he also reap". I have definitely reaped those consequences as you have seen.

The 20-21-year-old woman that I was in 2001 had simply gotten away from the will of GOD for her life. Even though I was raised in the church, I believed that I was not worthy of GOD's love, mercy and grace during that time of my life. That is where I went wrong. No matter what I do or what anyone does in life GOD loves you. Now there will always be consequences to our actions but GOD still loves you. I used to believe that because I was living a life of crime that he wouldn't hear my prayers. One thing that I learned that year was no matter how much of a sinner I was, when I called upon GOD in prayers or through my tears to help me, that is exactly what GOD did. In that rebellious year, GOD still came through for me. I learned that your relationship with GOD is between you and GOD. It is not limited to your attendance or what you do in a building structure we call the church.

My encouragement to any woman who may be experiencing the same kind of year that I had in 2001, is to continue to pray. GOD will hear you and he will answer. The most important thing you can do is have faith and believe that GOD will answer you. Hebrews 11:6 "But without faith it is impossible to please him: for he that cometh to GOD must believe that he is, that he is a rewarder of them that diligently seek Him". Hebrew 11:1 "Now faith is the substance of things hoped for, the evidence of things not seen." So even if you are in the midst of you storm and it looks like things are not going to go in your favor, continue to have faith. Even if you have a mustard seed. Just start speaking and declaring what you want to occur. Write in a journal your letters to GOD. Tell GOD how you feel and what you want to come out of your situation. You will be amazed how you will see the very things you prayed about eventually be manifested in your life.

As you believe in GOD remember to also believe in yourself. It doesn't matter what anyone else thinks about you. What matters the most is what you believe about yourself. Once I started to believing that I was more than that rebellious girl, more than a woman who would steal, more than a woman who sold drugs, more than a victim of an abusive relationship, more than a motherless daughter, more than the lowest part of my life, I realized that I am a woman of prayer. I am a woman of passion. I am a woman of purpose. I am more than I could have ever imagined to be. I am an example of a wonder woman for my daughter and I can show her a different way of life. Most importantly, I am the woman living out my destiny and the woman GOD has created me to be…..ME.

Ms. Danessa Seward is currently working in the corporate office of a large healthcare organization and for a financial and life Insurance company in St. Louis, MO. Danessa is currently attending a spiritual school learning about meditation techniques, concentration and dream interpretation. She is an Inspirational Coach and she has been a panelist at a Women Conference. She attended the University of Northern Iowa where she obtained her Bachelors of Science Degree in Business Administration: Management in 2010.

Workbook:Life

Creating a Vision Board.

Now that you have evaluated your life's goals, considered your passion, and prayed to God for direction on your purpose, it's time to put all those images together and Design+Your+Life. Vision Boards are a physical way to see what it is we desire. Place your Vision Board near your prayer and meditation area so you can constantly ask God to bless your dreams and goals.

What you will need:
+ Poster Board OR A Collage App on your smartphone or tablet

+ At least one hour of free time

+ A picture of yourself

+ Scissors, tape, glue

+ Stacks of old magazines or online photos

+ Markers

Directions:
1. Find a comfortable, relaxing workspace. One that will allow your mind to drift and focus on your dreams and goals.
2. Put on some music or sounds that take you to your "happy place"/
3. Search for imagines reflective of the life you aspire to live. Look for images representative of the type of employment, home, family, and leisure life you are working towards.
4. Place the image of yourself in the middle surrounded by the pictures you cut out or selected on your device.
5. Use your marker to write inspirational quotes, scriptures, or mantras.
6. Display your board where you will see it daily. If it is on a device, make it your screen saver.
7. Pray and meditate over your board DAILY!

Letters to my younger self

"Life can only be understood backwards; but it must be lived forwards."
— Søren Kierkegaard

Dear Lost Queen,

I decided to write you this letter in hopes of saving you some of the pain, hurt, frustration, confusion, and insecure moments I could have avoided if this letter had been written for me. It's about the beginning of a period in my life where I realized I was lost and the growth that led me to the peace I now have. I struggled for so long trying to figure out the best way to get this message to you without exposing too much of myself. I'm always waiting on the right time, the right words, always trying to fix one more thing or wait until another area heals… But I've realized that the conditions may never clear up and YOU, and your future, are much more important to me.

I grew up in one of those "everything that goes on in this house stays in this house" households, and that started the beginning of my journey to isolation. Well, now I have a choice, and it is my responsibility to make sure you don't go through yours alone. I was what could be considered a spoiled only child. I was sheltered and didn't lack much from a materialistic aspect. Yet I longed for something much deeper! My mom always expressed love and was the best mother to the capacity of which she knew how. (I love her to pieces and I'm forever grateful) What I needed, money can't buy: time, guidance and wisdom. Oh, and a consistent father!

It was just my mom and I that lived together, but my dad would pop in and out throughout the years when he could. He had a drug addiction that was very powerful and unfortunately sometimes overshadowed the phenomenal man he truly was at his core. He would sometimes show up in 6-8 month increments (or less), but then there were times he may disappear for a year (or more). There was always inconsistency. By the way, coming around didn't always mean he and my mother were back together, the communication may have come directly through me or my sister. I failed to mention I have five half-sisters, but one I'm very close to. Everyone knew how much we meant to my dad and he would truly treated us like royalty every second we were together, but unfortunately his presence was not always as pleasant for our mothers. The on and off again love affair that my parents shared affected me heavily, mentally and emotionally. Sadly, it affected me in so many ways, I'm still realizing some even today. There were so many things I witnessed that a child should never be exposed to. But the obvious is an extremely unhealthy relationship. Every detail about it was wrong and I recognized that early on. In most cases one would consider it crucial to a young girls understanding and development if she perceived this to be a "normal relationship", but that's not always true. As I previously stated, I understood that this was not healthy nor something that I desired, but it still subconsciously negatively affected every decision I ever made in regards to relationships. One of those decisions that have caused my life to be a consistent blur is when I got into a serious relationship with a girl. This took me deeper into my journey of isolation. It also began a journey to one of the worst identity crises you ever want to experience.

    Sigh! This is where all the confusion comes in, but it's what I hope influences you the most. I've been in church all my life, and you know this is something we are told is wrong and we should not be doing. (As if I really needed to be reminded of this). Throughout the relationship, I would constantly have random mood swings; happy one minute depressed the next, in love and completely irritable at the same time. These were all feelings I kept to myself. I was constantly battling with whether this feeling was right or wrong, and if it was in fact wrong, why did it sometimes not feel that way? Although I felt I was in love, I still felt a sense of uneasiness and sometimes heavy guilt and shame. Although I knew deep down it was wrong, I thought, surely God wouldn't allow something like this to happen and then have a problem with it. I say this because in comparison to what I had been exposed to, it was one of the most beautiful examples of love I'd ever witnessed. There were many times I felt convicted but for various reasons chose to continue doing what I thought made me happy. Inconsistently happy, but happy.

    In hindsight, I believe the relationship may have been a form of escape for me. It provided laughter when I needed it, comfort, and someone to confide in in those moments you feel no one understands you. I could not understand at the time why we had such a strong connection, as we had many differences. I guess that's the result of two broken people connecting. The relationship continued on and off for a while and every time it was "off" I was the initiator. I tried to convince myself that eventually all of the discomfort would disappear because we loved each other. However, if I'm honest, even when I did my best convincing, I always saw myself married with kids in my future. Throughout the relationship I dated guys when we were "off" but somehow always found myself back in that relationship. I was blatantly being disobedient and used love to justify it. Well, this caused me to hurt many people along the way, tell unnecessary lies, miss out on opportunities, and managed to confuse the hell out of myself. Most importantly, I disappointed God so many times, continued to distance myself from Him, and constantly hurt Him. When you have a relationship with God you know when you're doing something he's not pleased with, or he may have specifically told you not to do. Although I knew what his expectations were from me, I chose to ignore it.

    As a result of choices, I learned the hard way that deliberate disobedience is one of the best ways to silence God. I went through these phases where I would pray for guidance, confirmation on certain things, or just simple answers and I heard nothing. There was complete silence! This had to be one of the lowest, darkest places I have ever experienced. It wasn't until I became frustrated with confusion and completely overwhelmed that literally caused me to breakdown. It was in that moment that I realized what I was missing and decided that I didn't care how much someone meant to me, or how much they loved me, there is no relationship that I need more than God. So I decided to choose us! That was the beginning of my journey of discovery, restoration, and destiny.

There will still be times of uncertainty, fear, loneliness, temptation, and maybe even times where you take a few steps backwards; but if you continue walking you will eventually meet exactly what you need halfway. Do not let mistakes or people keep you from moving forward to freedom! Although there are many areas in my life that are still under renovation, I have never had more peace, such clarity, or experienced such healing. I'm not saying that what solved my situation will be the solution for everyone who has ever experienced a same sex relationship, but if anything about my story resonates with you, or if you personally feel like this is an area that hinders your relationship with God or causes stagnation in your personal development, then choosing God and allowing him to guide to is the only way. Stop comparing yourself to others and trying to figure out why you are being held accountable for things it seems others are free to do. Scared, confused, and possibly still in love, choose God. He will make provision for everything you lack, heal every part of you that's hurting, reveal the truth about every lie you've ever been told, and provide comfort and restoration in every moment of despair. I know everything is cloudy right now and you probably feel like you're more confused than any human being should be, but I promise, you will immediately begin to find your way again. Each day you will discover something new about yourself and all the beauty around you. Take back control over your life…..Destiny awaits.

Karayan Adia Willis is a passion driven young professional with experience in both personal and employee development. Ms.Willis is a native New Orleanian with an extensive background in the fields of hospitality,
business, management, and program development. She has served as a staff member and is currently serving as a mentor for youth empowerment non-profit organization Pinkhouse Inc. Karayan is very well balanced, and finds great happiness in her passion for travel, food, and music, but most importantly serving others.

Dear Beautiful Queen in the Making,

How I love you. I look and see potential, growth, possibility, liveliness, and dreams, all resting inside of you. You see the world in love, goodness, and truth; things that are normally erased or looked over by so much negativity and despair. I am writing you for many reasons, the first being that I love you. I love everything that God made in you. God created you fearfully, beautifully, wonderfully, truthfully, and divinely. Your creation was a breath of fresh air, a light that shines brighter than any other light. I love you, your spirit, and your heart. I desire to protect you, shield you from hurts and pains, and yet give you insight to not make some of the mistakes I made.

Your identity is in God. Never, ever forget that. Who you are, what you are and what you represent is in the Almighty God. Quite often you will find yourself questioning your abilities, your purpose, even your livelihood in comparison to what you see around you. For many years, I thought I wasn't beautiful. That God gave me the wrong body, face, and personality. I wanted to be "normal, cool, like everyone else", because I thought that was right. I looked to food, to money, even to my friends to give my identity a purpose, and all the while, I just had to look to my heavenly Father. When I finally reached the place where my tears were overflowing and flooding my heart, I reached up and took a hold of God's hand and he released that need to be "like everyone else". When you try to hold on to comparisons, it can cause you to look for who you are in places and people that are set-up to distract you. How can someone who was not created to be you, tell you how to be you? I implore you to see that God gifted you with everything you need to be the woman he has called you to be. Who you are inside and out, was created and envisioned by the one true and living God, and no friend, social media outlet, or "how to be poppin" write up can define what is inside of you.

    My love, I see the potential in you and I desire to protect you so fiercely. I don't want you to forget that your fulfillment is not, and cannot be found, in a man. It's always nice to have a special someone, a "boo", a "bae" that you can call, text, snuggle, cuddle, and fantasize about all day; but my princess, you are more than that. You are the good thing, the beauty, the prize, and don't you ever allow a man to make you think you are less than that. Your purity may be tested, your flesh may over take you, and you may fall into that temptation. Does that mean your crown is revoked and God is done with you? Absolutely NOT!!! I thought the same thing when I lost my virginity.

    I was in a relationship with someone I cared about and loved, and it was what I wanted to do. I honestly thought doing it would keep him, it would make him see that I was willing to do whatever it took to make him happy, even if that meant breaking my covenant with God. And I was at a crossroads, an impasse where it was either keep doing the sin or turn and go back to God for forgiveness. Can I be honest? I kept going back to the sin, and God kept pulling at my heart to come back to him. It caused me to withdraw from my friends, my job, even my prayer life, because I wanted the temporary pleasure from a temporary relationship. I pushed myself to the point where I even wanted to try to get pregnant, simply because I wanted an everlasting tie with him. Yep, I was crazy, and it was because I allowed my flesh to have rule over my body. I don't want that for you love. I want you to live freely, love completely, and know that sex cannot, will not, and should not keep a man. There's a happy ending to what happened to me. God blocked and protected me from pregnancy, sexually transmitted diseases, and soul ties. God ended that relationship and pulled me back to him because that's where I am supposed to be, and guess what; you are supposed to be with him too.

　Now, before I wrap this letter of love to you, I want to give you one more token of love: Remember to LIVE! This world is scary, sometimes intimidating, and often a little overwhelming. In the midst of all this, remember to live. To not allow fear to pause you from living in the moment, but seize the day and experience life. Go on adventures, see the world with your beautiful eyes, shoot, go out and dance in the rain! Live richly in the big and little moments, the smiles of others, and the hugs and kisses of loved ones. Live in the growth of yourself as a woman and in the manifestation of God's grace upon you and the love of Christ within you. I see the struggle of others, and I pray that as you read this through smiles (and possibly a few tears) you will see that you are loved, you are purposed in God, and what he has for you is beyond a million words I could ever write. I love you, I pray for you every single day, and most importantly I am proud of you.

With all of my love~
Ashley

Ashley, a native of Waterloo, Iowa, uses her voice to empower, encourage, and inspire other women to know their worth and walk in it proudly. As a proud member of Antioch Baptist Church, she serves as a worship leader, young women's ministry member, and choir director. Her desire to let other women know that no matter what, following your heart, and most importantly Christ, will lead you to your destiny and purpose!

Thinking back,

If I could tell my younger self anything it would definitely be to dream huge, but allow the little things to make you incredibly happy. To "wake up each day and look forward to what new and exciting opportunities are going to present themselves today." All of my life I've been the model child (Perfect Patty). Perfect grades, never got in trouble. Went to college, hair school, and opened a hair salon by the time I was 24. Life was good no true complaints. I began to look deeper into myself for my higher purpose. I meditated, did yoga, read self-help books and I was beginning to figure out how to manifest some of the things I wanted in life. I found myself in a not so great relationship but I figured all other aspects of my life were pretty good, so I'd be ok.

Then one day my life shifted. The tragic loss of my brother. It was something no one saw coming. It shook my entire existence up. I had no idea how I manifested something so devastating. The flow in my life was gone. I struggled day in and out trying to get that balance back in my life, but nothing worked. All of my old happy places became sad memories. Therapy didn't even help. Then one day I woke up and said I'm moving into my brother's condo. No one had been there since his murder which was right out front. I yearned for some peace in my life and was willing to take the leap of faith to try to find it. I moved in with the intentions making the best of every single day because I finally understood the phrase life is short. The present is a gift you've got to enjoy it. It was a big adjustment because it was my first time on my own in life. It was also the most exhilarating time of my life. I began to feel like I was completing his life by living my dreams. The fact that I was fortunate enough to enjoy the fruits of his labor brought me so much gratitude. It made me want to give more because I felt like I was given the ultimate gift of living. I had finally let other people's opinions of me be just that their opinions. I wasn't just existing anymore I was living. My negative friendships were beginning to fade away. Followed by meeting amazing new people. Business at my salon picked up drastically and I was able to start another side business. I truly enjoyed getting up and working on growing both of my businesses. My happiness began to pour on to my clients. People suddenly always wanted to be around me. They said my good energy was contagious. That made me feel good and kept me wanting to stay in that state of mind. Dream vacations were no longer distant but now attainable. I had finally began to dream big, but got excited about the little things in life. I've finally gotten to the point in life where all I really care about is enjoying life every single day.

Tammy Gardner is the Owner of the Arlington, Va. based hair salon As the Heads Turn II which also serves as a children's spa. Tammy is a licensed stylist with more than ten years of industry experience. In addition to
being an avid entrepreneur. This is evident through the launch of her Young Living business venture which inspires wellness, purpose, and abundance by distilling nature's greatest gifts into pure essential oils.

Dear Maureen,

You are disoriented and noticeably shaken. It is a fresh fall day in October and you have settled into your first job in the fashion Industry in New York City. Having recently moved from Philadelphia after your studies, and successfully landing a position and securing a new apartment, you are feeling pretty completed. However, here it is in the late afternoon on a Friday and you are sitting opposite your present boss being informed that your position is being cut due to money-planning.

What are you going to do? First, before packing your things, I need you to go to the bathroom and take a full breath. Comprehend that this nightmare has happened to a large number of other individuals in the country recently. In understanding this, it will ease the uncertainty you are feeling. You have the ability to take action. Rather than having your apprehension and fear lead to making nonsensical choices like surrendering your new apartment (which will later turn out to be wasteful) start the quest for low maintenance jobs to help with everyday costs. You live in New York City, opportunities abound. You will come to realize this fact as you wind up in numerous odd occupations in the years ahead (laughing).

Second, from today forward, repeat again and again, like your own little mantra: *Your presence is vital and you will manifest every single good thing that fits in with you*. Also, use this time to tap into your spirituality and trust God, that in all of this, he is ever present. In knowing this, your spirits will be immediately lifted.

For the next several years as the economy picks itself back up, jobs will come and go, and your career is going to be somewhat of an unfavorable uphill battle. There are moments even, when you could hear your traditional Haitian father asking if Fashion Design was an astute career move years prior. But in all this misfortune you'll find some great fortune when you finally start to realize that everything does happen for a reason.

Likewise, in this moment of having copious spare time, I need you to attempt new things. Inundate yourself in the things you didn't have sufficient energy and time to while in school. You will fortunately unearth jewelry making which will deliver a considerable measure of new and energizing open doors. Continue making mistakes, since you will inevitably learn not to stress to such an extent. Fully acknowledge your leap forward moments when they happen, no matter how enormous or how little, since they too are essential.

With high hopes for you always,
Maureen

Maureen Saturne is an adept Senior Technical Designer at an apparel company in New York City. Maureen wears many creative hats and also finds passion in designing and creating one of a kind jewelry pieces. After completing the Metalsmithing program at the Fashion Institute of Technology, she immediately began creating her own jewelry and selling her work online. She is heavily inspired by shape and embraces natural imperfections of the hand at work. Each piece of jewelry is made with care and given special attention to detail.

Chile...

You don't know everything! So please don't try to grow up to fast (enjoy your childhood). Listen to your intuition. Follow your dreams. Live your life for you. Be yourself. Eliminate the word "can't" from your vocabulary because you can do anything you put your mind to. Don't listen to the naysayers. Take risks. Explore opportunities. Experience life. If it's meant to be, it will be, so don't try to force it. Become financially literate early on (i.e. savings plan, create budget, retirement plan). Set goals and take the necessary step to reach them. Don't get comfortable in your situation. Seek to learn something new every day. Understand the difference between settling and settling down (love vs. lust). Don't try to play the victim because it's not about what happens to you in life but how you react to it.

Life will be nothing like you imagined it to be. Don't get me wrong, it will throw a lot of punches and curve balls at you. You will take some hard hits and experience some failures. But you will learn to roll with the punches and knock those curve balls out of the park. Don't regret any decision you make (good, bad, or ugly). Believe that your past will influence your present but it will not dictate your future. It will all work out in the end. It may not be when or how you want or thought it should, but it will be best for you. Remember, everything happens for a reason. When you make mistakes (trust me you will make many) take responsibility for them but make sure you learn, grow and evolve from every situation, experience, and action.

All of this advice became relevant when I decided to make the move to a new state. I moved here not knowing anyone or anything. I just stepped out on faith and decided to live my life for me in order to follow my dreams. I know I wanted more for myself, and at the time did not know what that was, but I knew it was not in my current location. Being hundreds of miles away from my family and not knowing anyone was a very difficult transition. Since I was a college student I didn't have the financial capabilities to just up and go. Therefore, I spent many holidays alone, missing out on family events, birthdays, and such. But I had goals that I wanted to achieve so I stayed focused and began to find outlets to keep my mind off being "alone." My drive and ambitions fueled my fire to pursue various opportunities. But, even after 7 years, I still have difficult days and struggle. The cliché saying "that nothing in life is ever easy" resonates in my head and drives me to push harder and not get comfortable or complacent where I'm at. So, I continue to take risks, pushing myself to develop my skills and abilities.

During my struggles, failures and opportunities, I have discovered my passions, and am currently a working model, dancer and actress; my dreams, that if I didn't step out on faith I probably would not have discovered. But I almost gave it all up last year when I developed adult acne and had a severe breakout. Now most teenagers deal with acne as their bodies go through changes, but as an adult this was a different story. My face is my career, so when this happened I thought my life was over. I wanted to throw it all away (modeling, dancing, and acting) and even went through a state of depression. I went to four different specialists and was prescribed multiple antibiotics from the dermatologist that ALL caused allergic reactions and made my acne worse. As a result, I stayed up countless hours at night researching what could be the cause of my breakouts. I changed my diet (stopped eating meats, sweets, dairy), my cleansing process, and even what I washed my clothes with, etc. I cried myself to sleep on many occasions and prayed to God, asking him why I was going through this situation. I stayed in the house for a straight week, missed various events, and opportunities because I did not want anyone to see me this way. It was tearing me up on the inside and although people were telling me it was going to be alright, I didn't listen. I wanted to rip my face off.

    I didn't like the negative thoughts I was having, so I began to pray when I wanted to cry. This lead me to research different solutions and I started to connect with other women who were going through the same things I was. By gaining a support system of others that were going through the same issues, I was able to discuss my frustrations, share my experiences, gain some encouragement, and began to gain back my confidence. Once I realized that something like this could happen to anyone and at any time, I changed my thought process. I began to think more positively about the outcome of this "adult acne breakout." I discovered how to love the skin I was in and recognized that people were drawn to me and loved me for my other characteristics (i.e. personality, sense of humor, intellect, etc.), not just the physical, outer surface. Shortly after I made this evolution, I noticed my face started to clear up.

    Honestly, I thank God that I went through this experience because it allowed me to truly look at beauty differently. I now notice and appreciate the inner beauty, not only in myself, but in others as well. It also helped to build my true confidence, which has helped me tremendously in the modeling field. This new found confidence allowed me to go into casting calls and not be intimated by the petite ladies, because I was a curvy, plus size woman. My confidence now exudes in my walk when I'm pumping out on the runway. And, it radiates through my eyes in photoshoots. They say everything happens for a reason. Therefore, I am grateful for all the ups and downs, growths and setbacks, life experiences, and lessons learned. I have experienced. God makes no mistakes and does not put more on us then we can bear. I said it before in the beginning but I want you to live by this saying that I have lived by for years and has helped me through many things...the past may influence the present it does not dictate your future.

Sincerely Your Older Wiser Self,

Kateea Scott

Kateea Scott is a risk taking, triple threat native of Waterloo, Iowa. Her modeling, acting, and dancing career begin to foster and flourish just shy of two years. As a model, during her first casting call, she knew that being a true role model for curvy plus size women was something she wanted to fulfill. She is passionate about helping, guiding, inspiring, and motivating individuals to reach their full potential. She is currently a HRD instructor at Randolph Community College, a vibrant fitness/dance instructor (KS Antics Style), and consistently working to be a confident and prosperous model, actress, and dancer. She also enjoys traveling, watching movies, cooking, and experiencing new things.

My dearest Lynn,

You look at your kids and not care, do not have any fight left in you. You walk miles stopping by your usual place you call your "Piece of Peace" wondering if you just jump in, is it deep enough? Imagining yourself driving head first into a semi, or praying, and pissed because you woke up. You began to look confused swallowing and continuing to fight back tears, trying to O.D. In 2000 you fell asleep not realizing you never took the pills.

People keep telling you to pray and you keep hearing the voice of momma, but the pain remains. Turning to temporary reliefs like sex, drugs, working, and singing, only gives you a moment of peace. You become distant and withdrawn from not only your friends, but family as well. The things that use to make you happy like being surrounded by people who love you, couldn't penetrate the thoughts that you have to rest permanently. Sitting around what use to give you joy only seem like pain, taking lots of work for you to feel anything. Childhood rejection, identity crisis, anxiety and depression becoming overwhelmed with the dark side of your life, you couldn't cope. You will find it difficult to ask for help, so instead you build the wall, and death becomes your friend.

Love has no meaning, jumping into a relationship after a messy divorce, you become numb to what love really is. Searching for ways to cope, finally, you feel like you're on top of the world. But, inside you were boiling over with fear and grief, loss of hope, and feelings of unprotection. You know the scriptures "no weapon formed against me shall prosper, come unto God and he will give you rest", but they are not in your heart. Pepping yourself up before anything even if it is simply going to the grocery store. Asking questions like what to wear, who will be there? Becoming paranoid about the things you do and being hard on yourself about doing something wrong, you reflect on your anger, losing control, and balance in your life. You began triggering selfless thoughts imagining yourself at the lowest of low. Not focusing and being unable to control your suicidal thoughts you become sad with yourself and start belittling yourself. Your relationship begins to spiral downward and more and more you begin to not want to exist. In a fit of tears you call Mama periodically telling her you are done mentally, emotionally and spiritually.

The altar is your sounding post for your pain, on your knees crying out until the words sounded like foreign tongues and your eyes swollen. This will make you feel renewed only for a moment, but you find another alter and do it all over again. Singing is your outlet but never your cure, although it helps to write and sing there are things you could never speak on. You will war on the inside and the only thing that seemed right was for you to disappear. Contemplating relocation, but the pain is not produced from the outside, but from within.

The breakdown of your body and memory started to slip, not to mention a divorce after 12 years of being with your husband. The desire of isolation sets in, but silence is the loudest sound because your thoughts never cease. One diagnosis after another will take a toll on you.

Financially stripped from every occurrence and knowing that facing another thing that will make you want to end it all. You feel that your upport circle has flat lined, and the flow of your life is at a standstill, as bad as cancer is running ramped and wiping us out like genocide. You pray that your next diagnosis would be a cancer so bad it would wipe you out. If you were stopped by the police you would hope, if I just go to jail for a few days I could sleep. Your mind feels invaded because what used to be this goofy, smiling, energetic woman, was now a broken, bitter suicidal little girl that wanted to go back in the womb where she was safe.

Life will teach you that it is impossible to go back into the womb but it was not too late to live. Before you understood that statement, you did not now you would hit rock bottom before it finally hit you. Your children will try to encourage you and give you back the words you gave them when they was going through. They will tell you how strong you are and how her strength comes from you. They will call and pray, or try to pray with, and for you, and tell you that you are more than a conqueror. Your mother will remind you of the things that you used to do along with your sisters and friends. The most mind boggling thing will be: you won't believe those words. Instead you will lean towards the negative then get in a relationship that you first believe will be your last, but the Most High will have a plan for you to be broken before you will be built up. Lynn, you will not realize that you are being called to surrender, being called to give up your will for His. You will decide that it was better to die than to live and that everyone will be better off without you. That decision will change your whole life....

Surgery after surgery, lie after lie, insult after insult and heartbreak after heartbreak, you concocted what you thought was your last drink, your last, what the kids call turn up. While alone, and after a long night of arguing and being broke down by someone who you looked at as your "God", you let everything out of you and began to cry out. Alone with your thoughts, silently screaming and with each sip you will pray to God. "Lord, I know I am going to hell. I know I failed you. Please take this cup from me. I am so tired Lord! I don't see no other way out of this. Now everyone will see my pain." The concoction will be so potent the first drink will have you dizzy. In the middle of drinking you will have a change of heart and your prayer will change. "Lord I don't want to die; I just want everyone to see how hurt I feel inside. Let me slip into a coma or just be hospitalized for a few months." You barely will be able to keep your head lifted. You will remember the times with your children, your mother's struggles, and your pain will build up through your eyes, blinding you with your tears. You'll drink every drop and find yourself passing out only to wake up many hours later with only swollen eyes from crying. "I thank you oh God! I praise you oh God! Thank you for sparing my life!" After that day and feeling loved by God, you will make it a mission to love yourself.

One round of rejection left and after that you will believe God opened up a new door that he has been waiting for you to walk through. When God elevates you, he takes you through a breaking process. Similar to a tryout. You are always a part of the team but you have to be tested for certain positions. With each test, you become stronger and wiser than before. After several tests it is up to you if you know Your test will come out of rejection in a way that will bring you to your knees. To love someone with your whole being and be rejected by them is a blow to your heart and your whole understanding. When God wants to hear from you and get your attention it is not always pleasant. The problem after your attempt to take your life was to hold on to a relationship that you thought would help you but man cannot save you, but God will save you but your test will be to see if you will run back to the concoction. Embrace the test and cry out, and pray to God. After that you will end up in Texas for 5 days, allowing yourself to feel all the pain of your entire life and finally be able to let go. Your shaven head will be a symbol of shame, freedom and new beginnings. The 5th day you will return home with a new you inside and out. Now the journey begins.

Taking pictures and being in front of people is normal for you. But this time around you see with new eyes. Morning affirmations to yourself will help you start your day. "I love you, you are beautiful and you will not entertain negativity," will be your pep talk to yourself. Greeting yourself with love every day while smiling at yourself in the mirror, will give you a boost that you need. Picking up a pen and being able to write words that were trapped inside you for years, will be like giving birth. You will release the pain onto paper and behind it will be great joy. Your smile will shine through your eyes and come from the inside, not just a painted canvas on your face. Your laugh will be so contagious that your children, family and those who knew and loved you will laugh along with you. It will feel like you are being celebrated because many did pray for you, but this time, you will feel their prayers over your life. You will feel alive again Lynn! Before the test you will give a testimony of how you attempted to take your life, never realizing God already had a plan and a celebration of your victory. From that testimony it will connect you with a beautiful woman who had her own battles and tests but won the battles and passed the tests. When you come back to reality you will give her a call and from that call you will become a Dream Coach for a program called Circles of Support. It is a program that supports other women who struggles with the weight of this world and comes together to make like easier by making friends on purpose. Helping them and them helping you reach goals in your lives without the exchange of money. After being able to come out of your shell and becoming a part of a community, you realize more of your worth and will expand what you were taught and your story. You will head a group you will name W.O.W. Women of Waterloo. It will be a movement of women empowering each other to help young adults in your community. You never seen this in your future when you were fighting with taking your life.

This is your story, there are many stories

that will be similar, but not your own. I know there are questions and these things you never knew you will go through. Lynn, never hold things like this in. I encourage you, my sister to always tell your story and share this with others. First you have to admit and see that there is a problem. There are so many women who suffer in silence because they feel like they are alone, no one has time for their problems or they feel they can handle it on their own. None of these is healthy thinking. Do not ride through this alone. Secondly, after admitting there is a problem, take time for you to heal and love on yourself. No one will love you next to God like you would. It might sound silly but get in the mirror and begin to say the things to yourself that you would like to hear from someone else. "Good morning beautiful! I love your eyes, I love that smile on your face," say it until you believe it. The saying fake it until you make it is oh so true. Be your best friend and take yourself out and enjoy yourself. Just be good to you. Lastly, you admitted the problem, took time for yourself, now help somebody else. Your battles and victories are not just for you but for someone else. Now that you have walked through hell and back find some other woman or young lady and help them through. When you feel alone, and don't think anyone will be around and need someone, remember those times and help someone else. Your words could be someone else's solution to a problem you already experienced. Support is important when you feel there is no hope because when you look into the world there is so much division and it says "it's all about me." We need each other to survive in this world.

Your most impacting time will be when you do something for yourself. You will not be pressured by the world to be something and someone you don't want to be. The love you have for yourself will be enough to have a reason to live again, to breathe again, and to be able to walk with your head high because you are a woman of worth. You will deal with the matters of your

heart. You will continue to speak into the lives of others through your life experiences. No women left behind is your goal, to reach women who are silently suffering and love them with your whole heart. Your tears will end up being tears of joy, tears flowing for those who have stopped crying, stopped trying, and for those who stopped living. You will mourn the ones who died in this cancer called suicide. You are beautifully and wonderfully made! A Queen that is full of royalty! You are more than a conqueror! Your victories have set a path for someone else to find the light in their darkness. I am now that light and it feels amazing! If you have people who are around you that say they love you ACCEPT the help. There are no overnight fixes but remember I say fake it until you make it. After a while you will believe the words you speak into your life. Freedom is being able to love yourself unconditionally, not be bound to what the world say love is. To thine own self be true Lynn and I love you. I wish I could lean over and hug you and tell you it will be easy, but it won't be. But I will tell you that your future is beautiful and you don't look like what you been through. I pass the baton of life and I whisper to your spirit "it's your turn, I am here waiting and cheering you on at the finish line. There is someone else waiting for you to help set them free."
I leave you with so much love,
Tanara

Tanara Lynnece Colson, a mother of 3 boys and 1 girl and 2 granddaughters and 1 on the way has a heavy background in music and a host of ministers in her family. Throughout her childhood and into adulthood, Tanara battled with many obstacles but always found a way to see the glass half full and reach her victories. Tanara's mission is to be transparent and reach out to every woman who is facing obstacles and need guidance on how to make it through it.

Letter to Your Younger Self

Take the time to write a letter to your younger self telling her the many things you wished you had known before life's realities began kicking in. Write from a place of love almost as if you were your own big sister, reminding yourself that joy always comes in the morning.

Dear Lovely,

Love,
Your Beautiful Self